SAMS
Teach Yourself
SAP R/3

Simon Sharpe

in 10 Minutes

SAMS

A Division of Macmillan Computer Publishing
201 West 103rd St., Indianapolis, Indiana, 46290 USA

SAMS TEACH YOURSELF SAP R/3 IN 10 MINUTES

Copyright © 1999 by Sams Publishing

International Standard Book Number: 0-672-31495-9

Library of Congress Catalog Card Number: 98-89582

Printed in the United States of America

First Printing: March 1999

00 99 98   4 3 2 1

TRADEMARKS

All terms mentioned in this book that are known to be trademarks or service marks have been appropriately capitalized. Sams cannot attest to the accuracy of this information. Use of a term in this book should not be regarded as affecting the validity of any trademark or service mark.

"SAP" is a trademark of SAP Aktiengesellschaft, Systems, Applications and Products in Data Processing, Neurottstrasse 16, 69190 Walldorf, Germany. The publisher gratefully acknowledges SAP's kind permission to use its trademark in this publication. SAP AG is not the publisher of this book and is not responsible for it under any aspect of press law.

WARNING AND DISCLAIMER

EXECUTIVE EDITOR
Bryan Gambrel

ACQUISITIONS EDITOR
Angela C. Kozlowski

DEVELOPMENT EDITOR
Susan Shaw Dunn

MANAGING EDITOR
Lisa Wilson

PROJECT EDITOR
Rebecca Mounts

COPY EDITOR
Pat Kinyon

INDEXER
Eric Schroeder

PROOFREADER
Kim Cofer

TECHNICAL EDITOR
Brian Bokanyi

INTERIOR DESIGN
Gary Adair

COVER DESIGN
Aren Howell

LAYOUT TECHNICIANS
Brandon Allen
Stacey DeRome
Timothy Osborn

CONTENTS

About the Author

A systems developer turned SAP training consultant with experience developing and delivering SAP training to various corporate clients, **Simon Sharpe** has 12 years of combined systems experience and has worked through several R/3 implementations.

Dedication

For my best friend Carol

Acknowledgments

Thanks to the editorial team at Sams. Your professionalism and attitude made me feel very much a part of a larger team. Thanks to Shirley Hollywood and Associates for my continued opportunities to work and learn on top-notch SAP projects.

WE'D LIKE TO HEAR FROM YOU!

As part of our continuing effort to produce books of the highest possible quality, Sams would like to hear your comments. To stay competitive, we *really* want you, as a computer book reader and user, to let us know what you like or dislike most about this book or other Sams products.

You can mail comments, ideas, or suggestions for improving future editions to the address below, or send us a fax at (317) 581-4663. For the online inclined, the address of our World Wide Web site is `http://www.mcp.com`.

In addition to exploring our forum, please feel free to contact me personally to discuss your opinions of this book at `bgambrel@mcp.com`.

Thanks in advance—your comments will help us to continue publishing the best books available on computer topics in today's market.

Bryan Gambrel
Executive Editor
Macmillan Computer Publishing
201 West 103rd Street
Indianapolis, Indiana 46290
USA

INTRODUCTION

SAP R/3 is an integrated business system designed to help organizations run such business processes as managing inventory, creating requisitions, processing sales orders, paying invoices, and so on. SAP R/3 covers a wide spectrum of business processes.

In the past, computer systems were specified and brought into organizations by each individual department: Human Resources chose its own system, Materials Management chose its system, Accounting chose its system, and so on. Although each system may have been the best choice for a particular department, keeping them working together was very expensive. This kind of complex patchwork system inhibited change in organizations—and we all know what happens to organizations that can't change quickly.

SAP R/3 provides a single integrated system to handle the needs of all departments in a corporation. This integration is the single biggest advantage to moving to SAP R/3. Its client/server architecture increases SAP R/3's versatility.

 Client/Server In client/server computing, part of the processing runs on your desktop PC (the client), and part runs on central shared computers (servers). The presentation and preprocessing is done on your PC; the information is stored on servers.

SAP R/3 consists of a series of application areas. Figure I.1 shows those areas and how they interconnect.

WHO IS *SAMS TEACH YOURSELF SAP R/3 IN 10 MINUTES* FOR?

This book is for anyone who fits one of the following descriptions:

- You want to learn quickly how to get the most out of SAP R/3.

- You are new to SAP R/3.

- You've learned only one SAP R/3 method and are looking for new ways to save time.

- You want to become more self-sufficient so that you can find your own answers rather than call your technical support team. (Because SAP R/3 is such a versatile product, each company can set it up in a different way. Therefore, you should look to your organization's support staff for job-specific training.)

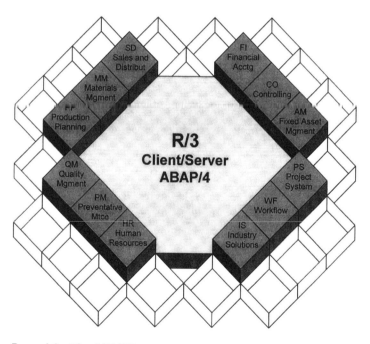

FIGURE I.1   The SAP R/3 system components.

NOTE TO CORPORATE TRAINERS

This book is an ideal starting point for training your staff on SAP R/3. You can even set up data similar to that used in the book on your training system and provide a handout of data that works at your site. The examples are all taken from MM, but the principles shown apply to all modules. Many companies use this book as a take-away from their basic navigation course.

- Chapters 1–12 give a good grounding in the basics.

- Chapters 13–24 offer tips to make users more productive.

- The appendixes offer a broad overview of all modules.

HOW TO GET THE MOST FROM THIS BOOK

Be aware that your screen might not match the examples in this book exactly. The screen shots in this book come from a number of hypothetical and demo systems; your system may be configured differently. For example, your company may not be using the SAP R/3 MM Purchasing module that's used as an example in the book (most *do* use MM). However, you can apply the concepts these lessons teach to other SAP R/3 modules.

Because SAP R/3 is so versatile, no two configurations will be the same. However, if you keep the following points in mind, you will be able to understand and use the information presented in this book and apply it to your own specific situation.

- Although SAP R/3 is accessible from various desktop computers, this book is based on Windows. You will need basic Windows skills to understand this book.

- You will get the most from the book if you sit down and work through the examples on your system.

- Where concrete examples are essential in this book, they are drawn from the Materials Management area around *Purchase Requisitions*. This is because purchase requisitions (used to control material purchases) are basic, easily understood business documents.

- SAP R/3 provides you with excellent guidance and help facilities. In fact, new users are sometimes overwhelmed by the variety and amount of information that SAP R/3 can provide. This book will guide you through SAP R/3 and show you how to take advantage of the help SAP R/3 makes available to you.

CONVENTIONS AND ICONS USED IN THIS BOOK

This book uses the following conventions to draw your attention to particular text (such as information you will see onscreen and information you'll enter into the system).

`Onscreen text`	Onscreen information appears in a special monospaced type.
What you type	Information you type appears in bold blue type.
Items selected	Commands, options, and icons you select (or keys you press) appear in blue type.
Menu title, Menu command	When referring to menu commands, this book uses the format menu title, menu command. Therefore, the statement "choose File, Properties" means "open the File menu and choose the Properties command."

In addition to those conventions, *Sams Teach Yourself SAP R/3 in 10 Minutes* uses the following icons to identify helpful information:

 New Term icons mark new or unfamiliar terms that are defined in "plain English."

Tip icons say, "Look here for ideas that cut corners and confusion."

Caution icons identify common trouble areas for new users and offer practical solutions.

Finally, some lessons include a "What You Need for This Lesson" reminder. Be sure that you meet the requirements listed there (which might include proper access to a particular screen or a previously created document) before you begin work on that respective lesson.

ACKNOWLEDGMENTS

Thanks to the whole team at Sams for their guidance, advice, and suggestions. You people are real professionals. Thanks to the team in the SAP Calgary office for providing me access to their system and for their comments and suggestions.

TRADEMARKS

All terms mentioned in this book that are known to be trademarks have been appropriately capitalized. Sams cannot attest to the accuracy of this information. Use of a term in this book should not be regarded as affecting the validity of any trademark or service mark.

"SAP" is a registered trademark of SAP Aktiengesellschaft, Systems, Applications and Products in Data Processing, Neurottstrasse 16, 69190 Walldorf, Germany. The publisher gratefully acknowledges SAP's kind permission to use its trademark in this publication. SAP AG is not the publisher of this book and isn't responsible for it under any aspect of press law.

LESSON 1

ACCESSING SAP R/3

In this lesson, you learn how to log on and off SAP R/3 and how to change your password.

 Say It Right   SAP is pronounced "ESS-AY-PEE"; it's not like the sap in a tree.

WHAT YOU NEED BEFORE LOGGING ON

Before you can access SAP R/3 from your PC, you need to take care of a few items:

- You must have the SAP R/3 client software installed on your PC. It's also called the *SAP GUI* (SAP Graphical User Interface, sometimes pronounced "SAP-gooey").

- You need to be connected to a network through which you can access your SAP R/3 server. You can usually arrange this through your local support organization.

- You need a user name and password to log on to SAP R/3. You can also arrange this through your local support organization.

- You need to know the client name of the system to which you want to connect.

Client Software   Programs on your PC that access information from an SAP R/3 *server computer* (a central computer that holds your SAP R/3 data files).

Network   A collection of PCs connected together. You may also be able to dial in to your network by modem to access SAP R/3 remotely or to access it through the Internet.

Working with Clients and Client Names

Many people misunderstand what the *client name* is. It's the name of the SAP R/3 system to which you are connecting.

Most companies have several clients designated for different tasks. For example, one hypothetical company has the following setup:

- The Client 401 Training system is used for training new users. Eventually, the training data is discarded. Purchase orders created here aren't issued, and the customer orders aren't filled. Therefore, this is a safe practice area.

- The Client 101 Production system is the live system used to run the business. It's not safe to practice here.

Use the Correct Client   Learn the name of your company's training system from your support organization and make sure that you're connecting to the system you need. It's frustrating to find out the work you intended to save was actually entered into the training system. Also, practicing on your company's production system can be a "career-limiting" move.

LOGGING ON

You can access SAP R/3 from various different desktop computers and software. Although the examples here are intended for Windows users, access from other operating systems will be similar.

You start from the Windows desktop. The first step of the actual process will vary from company to company, but there will be either an icon on your desktop or an item on the Windows Start button:

- If there's an SAP R/3 icon on your Windows desktop, double-click it to launch SAP R/3.

- If there's no icon on the desktop, click the Start button, move through the menu, and click the SAP R/3 menu item to launch SAP R/3.

Some companies also use an intermediate step, where you can make a selection from a list of available clients. Either way, the SAP R/3 logon screen appears (see Figure 1.1). This is SAP's "front door."

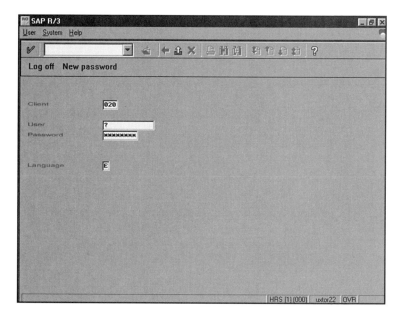

Figure 1.1   Type the client name, your user name, and your password to log on to SAP R/3.

Notice the screen title SAP R/3. The screen title helps you keep track of where you are in SAP R/3.

 Can't Find the Icon?   Some companies use customized SAP R/3 startup programs, and some name the icons after the project that initiated SAP R/3. For example, the icon might be called RMIS if your company installed SAP R/3 with a project named Retail Marketing Information System. If you don't see an SAP R/3 icon or an item on the Start menu, the SAP R/3 client software may not be installed on your PC yet. Call your local support organization to get help.

Follow these steps to log on to SAP R/3 from the logon screen:

1. Enter the number of your company's training system in the Client field.

2. Press Tab to move to the User name field, and then enter the user name you were given. (This is usually an abbreviation or a number instead of your full name.)

3. Tab down to Password and enter the password you were given. For security purposes, your password won't appear onscreen as you type it.

4. Depending on your company's setup, the Language field may or may not be filled in. If it is not, type **E** for English.

5. Press Enter to enter your information.

6. The first time you log on, the Change Password dialog box appears (see Figure 1.2), prompting you to change your password (for security reasons). Type your new password twice, making sure you type it the same way in both fields. Then click Copy.

7. Read the information in the SAP R/3 Copyright dialog box that appears, and then click Continue. The SAP R/3 home screen appears.

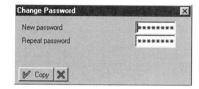

FIGURE 1.2   The Change Password dialog box.

Figure 1.3 shows the main SAP R/3 screen, where you'll start all your tasks and work. You learn about the elements that make up this screen in Lesson 2.

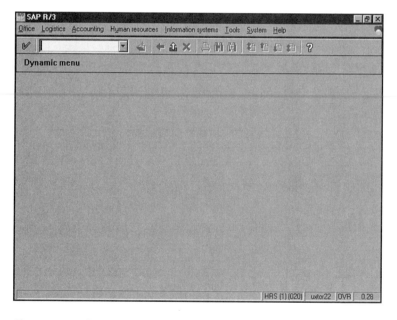

Figure 1.3   The SAP R/3 home screen.

PASSWORD PANIC

Remember these points about your passwords:

- Your user name and password authorize you to perform certain tasks. For example, if you are in Purchasing, your user name will probably allow you to perform only the tasks related to your purchasing duties.

- Some companies set up SAP R/3 with almost universal display access. This means that any user can look at virtually every record, except those of a sensitive nature.

- You will be given either a special temporary user name for training or your permanent user name right away.

- Be careful when choosing a password: You should protect it like your signature. Don't write it down or use words or names that can be guessed easily. (Combinations of letters and numbers are more secure.)

- Your password must be between three and eight characters long, and it can't start with three of the same character.

LOGGING OFF

To log off from SAP R/3, do one of the following:

- Click the Close (×) button on the SAP R/3 title bar.

- Press Alt+F4 (hold the Alt key and press the F4 key).

The Log Off confirmation box appears (see Figure 1.4). Click Yes to log off, or No to cancel.

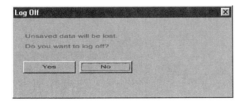

Figure 1.4 Do you really want to log off?

CHANGING YOUR PASSWORD

After the first time you log on, SAP R/3 won't present you with the dialog box to change your password. When you want to change your password again, go to the logon screen (refer to Figure 1.1). From there, follow these steps:

1. Enter the appropriate client name.

2. Enter your user name and your current password.

3. Click the New Password button near the top of the screen. The Password dialog box appears.

4. Enter your new password in both fields and click the Transfer button.

In this lesson, you learned how to log on and off SAP R/3, how to specify which client system to connect to, and how to change your password. In the next lesson, you will learn the components of the SAP R/3 interface.

LESSON 2

USING THE SAP R/3 INTERFACE

In this lesson, you see how to use the components of the SAP R/3 interface.

LOOKING AT THE SAP R/3 INTERFACE

As you learned in Lesson 1, "Accessing SAP R/3," when you launch SAP R/3, the SAP logon screen appears. Figure 2.1 shows the logon screen and points out the main elements of the user interface.

User Interface The controls and displays you use to operate something. In your car, for example, the user interface would consist of the steering wheel, the pedals, and the dashboard.

The title bar in this figure reads SAP R/3. This changes according to which screen you are looking at. The title bar also can help you confirm that you are where you need to be.

The menu bar contains a number of menus from which you select commands to perform your tasks. The available menus change depending on which screen you are in. Two selections available from all screens are System and Help. (You'll learn more about menus in Lesson 3, "Getting Around the Screen.")

Three standard Windows controls appear in the upper-right corner of the title bar:

- The **Window Minimize** control minimizes the SAP R/3 window to a button on your taskbar (where it remains active and you can

get to it easily). You can bring it back to full size by clicking it
or by pressing Alt+Tab.

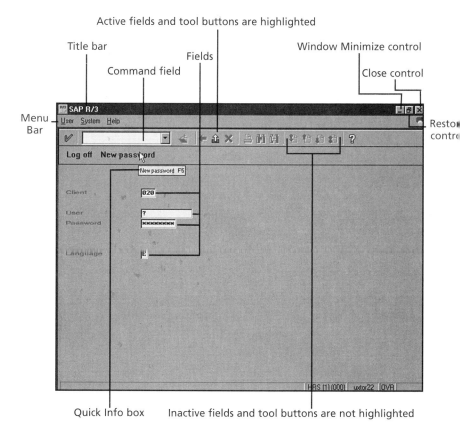

Figure 2.1   The SAP R/3 user interface.

• The **Restore** control changes your SAP R/3 session from occupying only a window on your screen to taking up the full screen.
You might want to use this to check information in another system (to check your email, for example) while using SAP R/3.
When your session is occupying only a window, the Restore
control is replaced with a Maximize button, which you can click
to make SAP R/3 take up the full window again.

- The **Close** control (×) shuts down your SAP R/3 session, after you confirm that this is really what you want to do.

The tool buttons across the top of the screen function as shortcuts you can use to perform common tasks. SAP R/3 displays active tool buttons in color; shadowed tool buttons don't apply to the active screen. (You'll learn more about the tool buttons later in this lesson.)

Figure 2.1 shows a Quick Info box labeled New Password F5. (These are also known as *ToolTips* in Windows 95/98.) These boxes appear when you position the mouse pointer over a button. This one, in particular, indicates that you're pointing to the New Password button, which performs the same function as the F5 key—both open the New Password dialog box.

SAP R/3 uses *fields* to accept and display information. Some things to consider when dealing with fields include the following:

- The length of a field shows you how many characters you can type in that field.

- The cursor (a flashing line or block) shows the field you are now in (the active field); anything you type appears in this field.

- SAP R/3 generally shows a field name for each field onscreen.

- When SAP R/3 displays a question mark in a field, you must enter something into the field before you can go any further. In the logon screen shown in Figure 2.1, for example, a user name is required. If you try to go on without filling in all the required fields, SAP R/3 gives you an error message.

SAP R/3 AND DIALOG BOXES

Sometimes SAP R/3 uses *dialog boxes* to display or request information. When a dialog box appears, it becomes the active window, and its title bar is highlighted.

Dialog Box   A box that SAP R/3 displays to communicate with you. Dialog boxes are smaller than the full SAP R/3 window.

Figure 2.2 shows the Change Password dialog box. Notice that its title bar is highlighted, and the main screen's title bar is no longer highlighted to show that it's not active. This means that only the dialog box is active. You can't access anything on the main screen behind it until you deal with the dialog box. You must click Copy or × (Cancel) to close this dialog box and return to the main screen.

This title bar is not highlighted   This title bar is highlighted

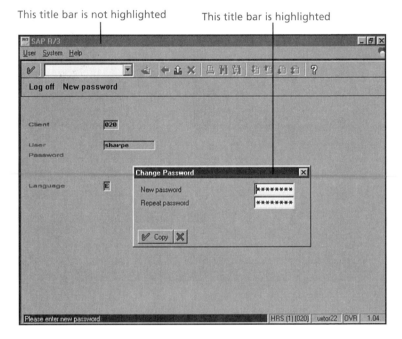

Figure 2.2   Only the dialog box is active.

Sometimes SAP R/3 presents you with several layers of dialog boxes. You must deal with those boxes to get back to your original screen.

THE SAP R/3 TOOLBAR

The SAP R/3 toolbar is the row of tool buttons across the top of the screen. Some buttons apply to all screens; others apply only to some screens. SAP R/3 tells you which are active by showing them in color. Shadowed tool buttons don't apply to the displayed screen. Table 2.1 shows you the tool buttons and describes each one.

Table 2.1   **SAP R/3 TOOL BUTTONS**

TOOL BUTTON	NAME	DESCRIPTION
	Check	Functions the same as the Enter key. When you click this, SAP R/3 checks the values on the screen. If all values are okay, you move to the next screen. If values are not acceptable, you get an error message.
	Save/Post	Saves the current record you are working with and backs out to the previous screen. SAP R/3 highlights any missing data when you click this button.
	Back	Backs you out to previous screen.
	Exit	Backs you out to previous level.
	Cancel	Aborts a process and discards the information.
	Print	Prints the current document.
	Find	Finds specified text or numbers.
	Find Again	Finds the next occurrence of the specified text or numbers.
		Scrolls to the top of the screen.
		Scrolls up one screen.
		Scrolls down one screen.
		Scrolls to the bottom of the screen.
	Field-Level Help	Tells you how SAP R/3 uses this field.

Back and Exit   New users sometimes find this confusing. If you are at the first screen in a series, the Back and Exit buttons will do the same thing. If you are at the third screen in a process, Back takes you back to the second screen, and Exit takes you right out of the process.

THE STATUS BAR

The status bar is usually displayed at the bottom of the SAP R/3 screen (see Figure 2.3). If your screen doesn't show the status bar, go to Lesson 19, "Customizing Your User ID," to see how to display it.

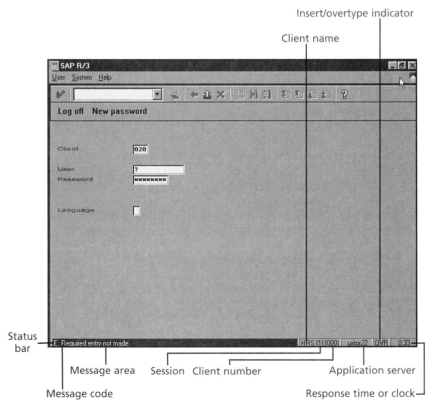

Figure 2.3   The SAP R/3 status bar keeps you informed.

SAP R/3 uses the status bar to pass along information. In particular, the message area part of the status bar contains a message preceded by one of the following codes:

CODE	MEANING
I	Information
W	Warning
E	Error
A	Abnormal end

In Figure 2.3, the status bar message E: Required Entry not made is an error notice telling you that you need to fill in a field before you can proceed.

Status Bar Error Messages   New users sometimes don't notice error messages on the status bar and don't know why they can't go on. The first thing you should look at when you have a problem is the status bar.

On the right end of the status bar, you'll find the following information:

- *Server name*—This is different from the one you typed in to gain access to the system, which may seem a little awkward at first. In Figure 2.3, the name is HRS(1)(000); HRS is the name of a demonstration system in the SAP Calgary office. We used the client code of 000 to access this system.

- *Session number*—You can have more than one SAP R/3 session open at once. See Lesson 18, "Using Transaction Codes," for details.

- *Insert/overtype indicator*—This indicates which typing mode you are in. You switch between insert and overtype modes when you press the Insert key.

- *Clock*—SAP R/3 provides a clock in the lower right corner. (You can also use this area to display the system response time. See Lesson 19, "Customizing Your User ID," for details.)

In this lesson, you learned the basics of the SAP R/3 user interface. In the next lesson, you see how to use the SAP R/3 screen elements to move between screens.

LESSON 3

GETTING AROUND THE SCREEN

In this lesson, you learn how to get around the SAP R/3 screen and how to get help on the fields displayed.

USER REQUIREMENTS FOR THIS LESSON

To understand the examples in this lesson, you will need either a user logon name with authority to create a purchase requisition, or an *application area* where you have authority to create another *document*.

Application Area   An area in SAP such as Purchasing, Human Resources, Plant Maintenance, and so on.

Document   The generic name for a standard business form. Although you may be used to thinking of a document as paper, in this sense it refers to an electronic business transaction record. A purchase order is a document, as are a maintenance request and an invoice.

The example used in this lesson is a purchase requisition, which is typical of many other business documents. If your user name doesn't give you the authority to create a purchase requisition, find out what you do have permission to create and use that document as your example.

Unauthorized Documents It doesn't do any harm to try to create a document that your user name isn't authorized for. You will, however, get an error message on the status bar.

GETTING TO AN SAP R/3 DOCUMENT ENTRY SCREEN

All business transactions involve documents. Sometimes SAP R/3 creates documents automatically, but at other times you need to create documents yourself with a document entry screen. Document entry screens exist in all modules.

No matter what kind of document you want to create, you begin at the SAP R/3 home screen (refer to Figure 1.3 for a refresher). To access the purchase requisition document entry screen, follow these steps:

1. Choose Logistics, Materials Management (see Figure 3.1). Notice that some commands have a small arrow beside them, which means that choosing the command will display more choices on a submenu.

An arrow means that a submenu will appear

Figure 3.1   Going to Purchasing.

2. Choose Purchasing. The Purchasing screen appears.

3. From the Purchasing screen, choose Requisition, Create. The Create: Purchase Requisition: Initial Screen appears (see Figure 3.2).

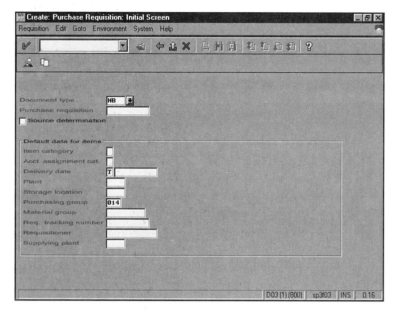

Figure 3.2   You're ready to create a purchase requisition.

 Two New Buttons   The buttons that show mountains and pages (in the upper-left corner) vary from screen to screen. To see what they do, point to them. In this case, they are Item Overview and Copy Reference. Item Overview shows the "summary" screen of a document. Copy Reference allows you to copy the details from another document into the one you are creating.

 It Doesn't Look Like That   In this example, some of the fields appeared with values already in them. You could have different fields carried in. See Lesson 16 to carry some values in for yourself. You can type over any value that is different from what you need.

4. Notice the little box to the left of Source Determination. This is called a *selection box* because a mark inside the box indicates that the function is turned on; a blank box indicates that the function is turned off. For this kind of document (purchase requisition), you could choose whether you want SAP R/3 to automatically determine the source of the material. For now, leave this box blank. Press Enter; the document entry screen appears.

Figure 3.3 shows the Create: Purchase Requisition: Item Overview screen. It's typical of the many document entry screens in SAP R/3.

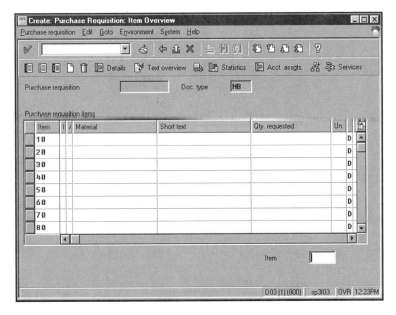

Figure 3.3   One view of the purchase requisition document entry screen.

Is yours different? Two different views of this screen are actually available. Choose Edit, Change Display to switch between the two formats. I prefer the "stacked" display (see Figure 3.4), where I can see all the fields onscreen. All exercises in this book show the stacked display.

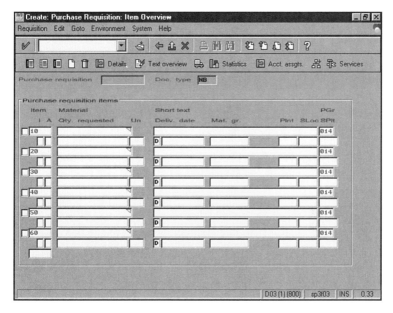

Figure 3.4   The "stacked" view of the purchase requisition document entry screen.

Many business documents have a single *header* and multiple *line items*. You can use this screen to enter a purchase requisition with one or more line items. You can request several kinds of products on a single purchase requisition. Each product will be listed as a single line item.

 Header   Information that's common to all line items. On a cash register receipt, for example, the header contains the date, store, and so on.

Line item   One or more items that are part of a larger single document. In the cash register receipt example, the line items designate items, prices, and quantities.

In Figure 3.4, you can see the Purchase requisition and Doc. type header lines at the top. Because you haven't yet created a requisition, the Purchase requisition field is currently blank.

Also note the following things in Figure 3.4:

- The fields for each line item are *stacked* (there are two screen lines to contain each line item). The titles are stacked above the two lines in a pattern similar to the stacking fields themselves.

- There are selection boxes to the left of each line item. You will use these later to select a particular line item with which to work.

- Because of the way the fields are stacked, some displayed titles are very short (like the A field). See the later section "How the Fields Are Used" to learn how to get more details about any field.

GETTING AROUND AN SAP R/3 DOCUMENT ENTRY SCREEN

You can move around a document entry screen by using any of the following methods:

- Press Tab to see how the cursor moves from field to field. You can Shift+Tab (press and hold Shift and then press Tab) to move back through the fields.

- You can move to any specific field by clicking it.

- Within a field, use the cursor left and right keys to move around in the text you create.

- While typing in a field, you can use the Backspace or Delete key to remove characters. Backspace removes the character to the left of your cursor; Delete removes the one to the right.

OTHER WAYS OF GETTING AROUND

You can also use function keys on SAP R/3 screens. You don't need to learn these keys because all the functions are available with the mouse. However, experienced users sometimes find it more convenient to use function keys.

To get a list of active function keys for a screen, press Ctrl+F. SAP R/3 displays the list of function keys (see Figure 3.5).

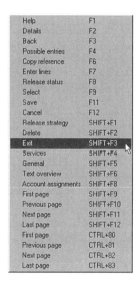

Help	F1
Details	F2
Back	F3
Possible entries	F4
Copy reference	F6
Enter lines	F7
Release status	F8
Select	F9
Save	F11
Cancel	F12
Release strategy	SHIFT+F1
Delete	SHIFT+F2
Exit	SHIFT+F3
Services	SHIFT+F4
General	SHIFT+F5
Text overview	SHIFT+F6
Account assignments	SHIFT+F8
First page	SHIFT+F9
Previous page	SHIFT+F10
Next page	SHIFT+F11
Last page	SHIFT+F12
First page	CTRL+80
Previous page	CTRL+81
Next page	CTRL+82
Last page	CTRL+83

Figure 3.5   The function key list.

You can also call up this list by right-clicking anywhere on the SAP R/3 screen. (The list that appears varies from screen to screen, depending on what functions are available.) Click an item in the list to select it.

Keyboard Convenience   If you're using a laptop and don't want to bother with the mouse, you can use SAP R/3 from the keyboard. Activate the menus by pressing F10, use the cursor keys to highlight your selection, and then press Enter.

HOW THE FIELDS ARE USED

Move the cursor to the Material field and click the Field Level Help button on the toolbar. (See Lesson 2, "Using the SAP R/3 Interface," for information on toolbar buttons.) SAP R/3 displays a dialog box that tells you how to use the field (see Figure 3.6).

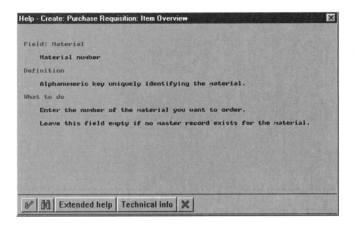

Figure 3.6   Field-level help.

Sometimes SAP R/3 uses fields in different ways for different kinds of records. For the purchase requisition in the Material field, for example, you could be buying a material that your company commonly buys. In this case, somebody in your company may already have created a *master record* for this material. For a material that already exists on your system, you would enter a material number. For a one-time purchase of a material, you would leave the Material field blank.

Master Record   Examples of master records are lists of products (material master) and lists of customers (customer master). (The dialog box in Figure 3.6 tells you to leave this field blank if the item you're buying isn't listed in your material master file.)

Sometimes a term displayed in the field-level help dialog box is highlighted. You can click a highlighted word to get a definition of it. Click
the highlighted word material. Figure 3.7 shows the definition screen
that appears.

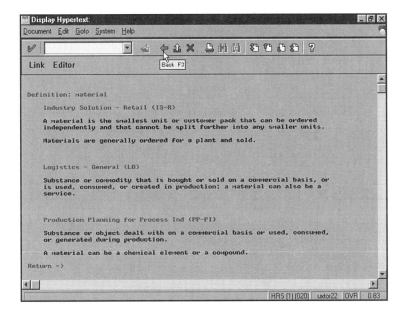

Figure 3.7 A definition screen.

When you finish reading the definition, click Back to clear the definition
screen. To exit the field-level help dialog box, click Cancel.

In this lesson, you learned how to get around on an SAP R/3 screen and
how to get help with fields and definitions. In the next lesson, you learn
how to move between SAP R/3 screens.

LESSON 4

MOVING BETWEEN SCREENS

In this lesson, you learn how to scroll around an SAP R/3 screen and how to move between screens. You also learn about the menus available on various screens.

USER REQUIREMENTS FOR THIS LESSON

To work through this lesson, you will need one of the following:

- A user logon name with authority to create a purchase requisition

- An application area where you have authority to create another document

THE DIFFERENCE BETWEEN BACK AND EXIT

The Back button (the arrow pointing left) and the Exit button (the arrow pointing up) both move you back through your work to a screen you viewed earlier. Work through the following steps to learn firsthand the difference between the two:

1. As you learned in Lesson 3, "Getting Around the Screen," go to the Create: Purchase Requisition: Item Overview screen.

2. Click the Back tool button. You are returned to the Create: Purchase Requisition: Initial Screen. (You haven't left the

process of creating a Purchase Requisition; you've simply *backed up* to an earlier screen.)

3. Press Enter to go forward to the overview screen again.

4. From the overview screen, click the Exit button. The first purchasing screen appears. In this case, you have *exited* the process of creating a purchase requisition.

5. Click Exit as many times as necessary until you get to the starting SAP R/3 screen. If you go too far, SAP R/3 displays a dialog box asking if you want to log off (see Figure 4.1).

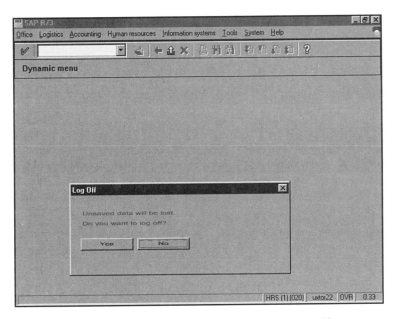

Figure 4.1 If you click Exit enough times, you can log off.

  If You Get Lost...   You can always get back to the initial SAP R/3 screen. Simply click the Exit button several times, and—no matter what—you can get back to a place you know. You will know you are on the main screen by its title, "SAP R/3."

6. If the Log Off dialog box appears, click Yes to log off, or click No to cancel the Exit command. (For our purposes, click No.)

 Use the Close Button   You can log off SAP R/3 from any screen by clicking the Close (x) button.

SCREEN BUTTONS AND SCROLLBARS

To learn about screen buttons and toolbars, you can go into Release Notes. (You don't really need to know anything about the Release Notes themselves, but they provide a convenient example that all users have access to.) Follow these steps:

1. From the initial SAP R/3 screen, select Help, Release Notes. The Find Release Notes screen appears. Note that it has three screen buttons: Complete List, Key word search, and Attributes.

 Screen Buttons   The buttons that appear in the row below the toolbar. You can click any of these buttons to get to another screen or to launch other processing. Screen buttons vary from screen to screen (unlike the toolbar buttons, which stay the same all the time).

2. Click the Complete list button, and the Display Structure: Complete List of Release Notes Available screen appears (see Figure 4.2).

3. Click the arrow beside Release Notes to "open up" that topic. (Clicking the arrow displays a topic's subtopics. Clicking the up arrow closes the topic again.)

4. Keep clicking arrows until you get to a screen that looks like the one in Figure 4.3.

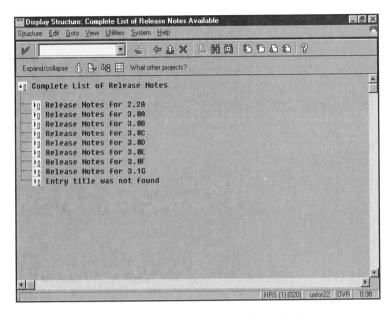

Figure 4.2   The Display Structure screen is like a table of contents to a much larger document.

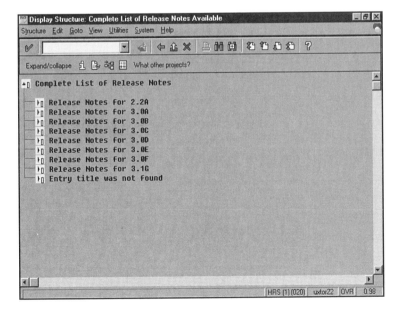

Figure 4.3   Several levels of a list.

5. The titles that don't have arrows have no subtopics. Double-click an individual topic to read its text. Figure 4.4 shows an individual topic.

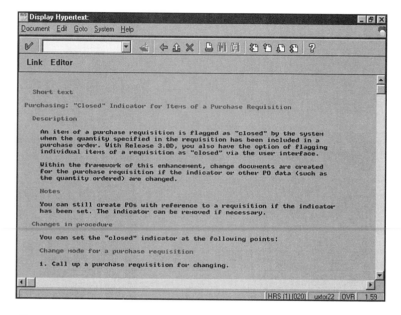

Figure 4.4   Open a topic and read the information on it.

Notice the scrollbars that appear along the bottom and right sides of this screen. They are designed to make navigation of a large document easier. Read on to learn how to use the scrollbars.

SCROLLING AROUND A SCREEN

Sometimes, the text to be displayed is wider (or higher) than your screen. Sometimes it's both. You can use several tools to scroll around in your document.

When the list is longer than your screen, use these methods to move down (and do the opposite to move up):

- Move down a full page by pressing Page Down on the keyboard.

- Move down a full page (or to beginning or end) by clicking the scroll buttons on the toolbar.

- Move down a full page by clicking in the scrollbar below the scroll box.

- Move large amounts by dragging the scroll box downward (press and hold the mouse button, and then move the mouse). When you release the mouse button, the screen display moves down.

- Move down one line at a time by clicking the down arrow that appears at the bottom of the scrollbar.

When the document is wider than your screen, you can use the horizontal scrollbar in a similar way to scroll left and right.

 No More Scrolling   When you can't move your scroll box down any further, you know you're at the bottom of the document.

UNDERSTANDING THE MENUS

Whereas scrolling allows you to move around within a document, menus allow you to move between screens. You learned in Lesson 2, "Using the SAP R/3 Interface," that the menu bar is the line just below the title bar in the SAP R/3 screen. The following three menus exist on every screen for your convenience:

- *System*—This menu gives you access to system functions.

- *Help*—SAP R/3 makes plenty of clearly written Help screens available online. Lessons 5, "Using Basic Help," and 6, "Using Task-Level Help," cover basic and advanced online help.

- *Options*—It's easy to miss the user options menu, which is marked only by a colored logo at the far right of the menu bar. This menu controls your user ID and is covered in more detail in Lesson 19, "Customizing Your User ID."

Figure 4.5 shows each menu and the commands they contain.

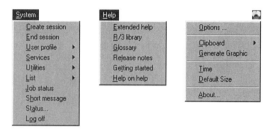

Figure 4.5   These menus are always accessible.

 Time or Response time   The fourth option on the Options menu is either Time or Response time. By selecting this option, you can toggle the time display at the bottom-right corner of your screen.

SAP R/3 provides several other menus. As you may have noticed, however, the other menus in the menu bar change according to the task you're performing. Those menus include the following:

- *Object*—This is usually named after the kind of document you are creating. In this case, it's the Requisition menu.

- *Edit*—This has commands for things you can do to the current object (such as Copy, Paste, or Select).

- *Goto*—Several screens are usually associated with each object. The Goto menu gives you one way to move between those related screens. In addition, commands on this menu are often duplicated on the screen buttons, which gives you two ways to get there.

- *Extras*—Sometimes an object's main screen contains all the commonly used fields, while less commonly used fields appear on different screens. The Details menu takes you to these screens.

- *Environment*—This menu allows you to work with other data associated with the current object.

- *View*—This menu allows you to select one of several views of your data.

Figure 4.6 shows each open menu. Take a good look at which commands are located on which menus. The submenus will also vary with the task you are doing.

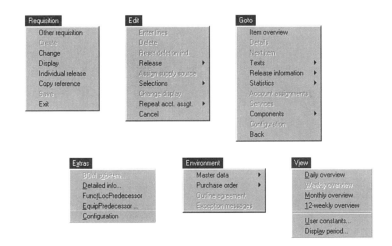

Figure 4.6   These menus change from screen to screen.

    Grayed Selections   A grayed option isn't currently available. For example, you can't save a record if there's no data in it, so the Save option might be shadowed.

    You Have Different Options?   Like most everything about SAP, the menus can be configured so that any company can add custom functions to any menu. Some companies add specialized menus for custom software they have built.

In this lesson, you learned how to move from screen to screen and how to use screen buttons, scrollbars, and multilevel lists. In the next lesson, you learn how to use the extensive Help facilities that SAP R/3 provides.

Lesson 5

Using Basic Help

In this lesson, you learn how to find the kind of help that applies across all SAP R/3 modules.

Online Help in SAP R/3

SAP R/3 provides two kinds of online help: basic help (which you learn about in this lesson) and task-level help (covered in Lesson 6, "Using Task-Level Help"). Learning how to make the most of both types of help will move you much closer to becoming a self-sufficient SAP R/3 user.

 Online Help Manuals and help systems that are distributed and accessed electronically instead of on paper.

Where to Start with Help

The first help you should look at is the basic help that "getting started" provides. While you are learning to use SAP R/3, you may need to check this kind of help from time to time to remind you how to use parts of the SAP R/3 user interface. To use the basic help system, follow these steps:

1. From the SAP R/3 screen, select Help, Getting Started. SAP R/3 displays a help window, similar to that shown in Figure 5.1. (The Help menu is available from any screen in SAP R/3.)

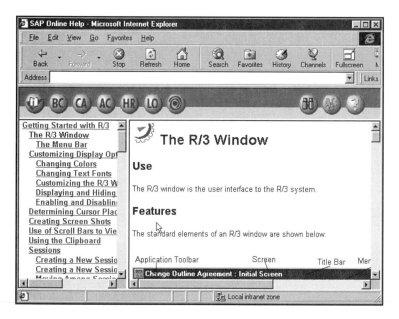

FIGURE 5.1   The first basic help window.

Not Quite the Same?   SAP R/3 help got a major facelift for version 4.0, going to a Web-browser style interface, as shown in Figure 5.1. Your help window may be presented in a slightly different style from that presented here.

Two windows   The left pane is the index; the right pane is the Help file.

2. Use the vertical scrollbar in the right pane to move down until you see a screen like the one shown in Figure 5.2. You can visit this section of Help whenever you need a refresher.

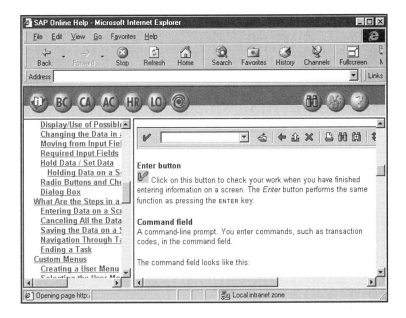

FIGURE **5.2**   SAP explains how you can use the interface.

3. Click the round button LO to move into the Logistics section of the SAP R/3 help system.

4. Use the vertical scrollbar in the left pane to move down through the index. You can click any items in the left pane to open the help text in the right pane (see Figure 5.3).

SEARCHING THE HELP FILES

Sometimes, the help you need isn't displayed in either window. You can use the search feature to locate this information:

1. From any help window, click the Search button (binoculars) below the menu bar.

2. Fill in the text of the item for which you want to search.

FIGURE 5.3   Zooming in to help on Logistics.

THE GLOSSARY

Sometimes listening to people talk about SAP R/3 is like listening to a conversation in a foreign language. To understand what they're talking about, you can access a glossary through SAP R/3's help system (see Figure 5.4). Follow these steps:

1. From any SAP R/3 help screen, click the round Glossary (ABC) button.

2. Click the letter (on the alphabet shown on the top) of the word you need defined.

3. Scroll down the left pane until you see the word you need defined.

4. Click the word to bring up the definition in the right pane.

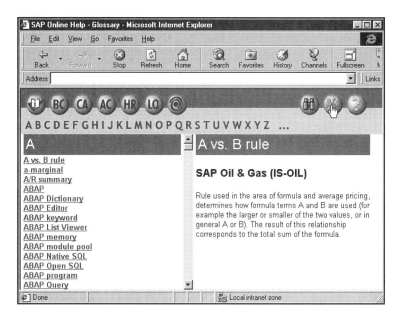

FIGURE **5.4**   Sorry, I don't speak SAP. What does that mean in English?

GETTING HELP ON MESSAGES

Sometimes, the messages that SAP R/3 displays on the message line aren't clear to all users. If an onscreen message confuses you, follow these steps:

1. Anytime SAP R/3 displays a message, double-click it for more explanation. SAP displays a more detailed version of the error message in a pop-up window.

2. After you read the message, click Close to remove the pop-up window.

In this lesson, you learned how to use SAP R/3's basic help, glossaries, and message help. In the next lesson, you learn how to use task-level help.

LESSON 6

USING TASK-LEVEL HELP

In this lesson, you learn how to find specific detailed help on tasks you need to perform in SAP R/3. You also see how to use context-sensitive help and to search the SAP R/3 Help Library for yourself.

WHAT YOU NEED FOR THIS LESSON

To practice using context-sensitive help, you need one of the following:

- A user name with the authority to get into the Purchase Requisition screen
- Authority to get into another document-creation screen so that you can follow along

This lesson assumes that you worked through the previous lesson and know how to use the browser-based help.

WHAT TASK-LEVEL HELP CAN DO FOR YOU

SAP R/3 provides detailed step-by-step instructions on how to complete *all* tasks (such as creating a purchase requisition or changing a work order). Because SAP R/3 is a generic product used in different ways by different businesses, the detailed help it provides is also generic and covers features that you may never need to use where you work.

Company-Specific Instructions   If your organization provides guides on how to perform certain tasks on SAP R/3 where you work, those guides will probably be more specific than the SAP R/3 help system.

GETTING TO THE RIGHT HELP MODULE

You can get to the help module you need in two ways:

- By using context-sensitive help

- By finding your own way in through the R/3 Help Library

Context-Sensitive Help   In this type of help system, the kind of help window SAP R/3 shows you depends on which screen you are in when you ask for help.

GETTING IN BY CONTEXT

For this lesson, assume that you're looking for help related to creating a purchase requisition. To access context-sensitive help, start on the Create: Purchase Requisition: Initial Screen. (If you don't remember how to get there, refer to Lesson 3, "Getting Around the Screen.") From that screen, choose Help, Extended Help.

SAP R/3 checks to see which screen you are in and takes you into the appropriate help module. In this case, because you're on a Create: Purchase Requisition screen, SAP displays help information on maintaining requisitions (see Figure 6.1).

Extended Help   This menu option is available no matter where you are in SAP R/3. The information it provides varies depending on where you are.

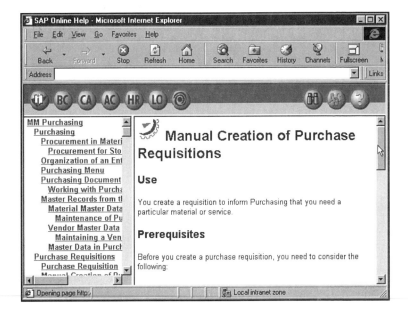

FIGURE 6.1   A task-specific help topic.

GETTING IN THROUGH THE R/3 HELP LIBRARY

Context-sensitive help works well if you know how to get to the screen for which you need help. If you aren't sure even where to start, you need to find your way in through the SAP R/3 Help Library. The following steps walk you through doing just that:

1. From any SAP R/3 screen, choose Help, R/3 Library. SAP R/3 displays the Library Manager screen, similar to that shown in Figure 6.2. Take a few moments to look at the options.

Library Manager   This library contains an amazing amount of useful, well-written information. Because it's online, it's easy to search, and you don't have to bother trying to keep it up-to-date like you do paper manuals.

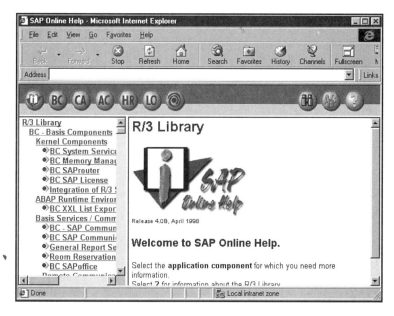

FIGURE **6.2** The information here is word-for-word the same as the printed manuals you can order from SAP.

2. To find help on creating a purchase requisition, click the round Logistics button, LO.

3. Scroll down the left pane until you get to MM Purchasing. Each subdocument is shown nested in its parent folder (see Figure 6.3).

4. Scroll the left pane down further and click Manual Creation of Purchase Requisitions.

5. A more detailed help screen appears (see Figure 6.4). If it looks familiar, it should—it's the same screen you saw for context-sensitive help in Figure 6.1. *The Help Library and the context-sensitive helps are just different paths to the same help files.*

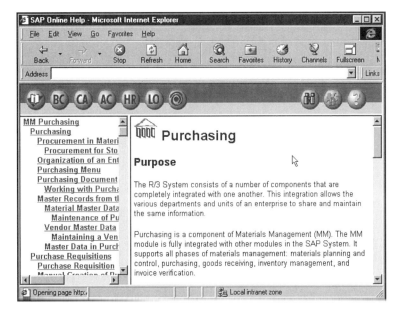

FIGURE **6.3**   An index to the Purchasing topics.

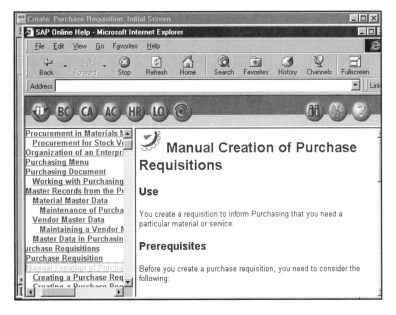

FIGURE **6.4**   You can click any of these items to see more detail on
them.

General Topics   Don't underestimate the value of such general topics as Master Data in Purchasing. Topics such as this give background information that will help you understand the way work flows through the system. (These topics aren't easy to find unless you enter the help system through the Library Manager.)

6. Click Creating a Purchase Requisition With a Master Record. The screen in Figure 6.5 appears.

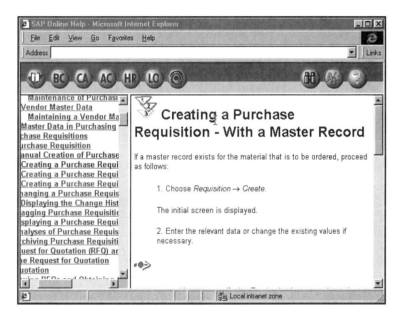

FIGURE 6.5   Step-by-step instructions exist for all tasks.

This exercise showed you that SAP R/3 provides a wealth of online help that you should dip into whenever it's needed. If you use only context-sensitive help, you may not see some of the other useful topics available in the SAP R/3 Help Library (such as the general topics).

In this lesson, you learned how to get step-by-step help on specific business processes. You also learned how to take advantage of context-sensitive help and the SAP R/3 Help Library. In the next lesson, you learn how to create a business document.

LESSON 7
CREATING A DOCUMENT

In this lesson, you learn how to create a business document, relying on SAP R/3 to help you through the process.

USER REQUIREMENTS FOR THIS LESSON

For this lesson, you need one of the following:

- A user logon name with authority to create a purchase requisition

- Another application area where you have the authority to create a document, so you can follow along

The examples in this lesson use a purchase requisition as the sample document. It's typical of other documents you create on SAP R/3. To create this requisition, you need to know:

- A material number in your organization that's valid at the plant for which you're requisitioning it

- A purchasing group in your organization that can buy for the plant you're using

CREATING THE PURCHASE REQUISITION

1. From the SAP R/3 screen, choose Logistics, Materials Management, and then Purchasing. The Purchasing screen appears.

2. Choose Requisition and then Create. The Create Purchase Requisition: Initial Screen appears. (You first saw this screen in Lesson 3, Figure 3.2.)

3. This screen allows you to create several kinds of purchasing documents. To create a standard purchase requisition, enter **NB** in the Doc. Type field.

4. Press Enter. If your company's configuration doesn't include a required entry for requisition number, the Create Purchase Requisition: Item Overview screen appears (see Figure 7.1). If you press Enter on a screen that requires values, SAP R/3 prompts you for the missing values.

Different Strokes   Most companies want SAP R/3 to assign the purchase requisition numbers and set it up to do just that. Other companies may want to assign the numbers manually.

Different Display?   If your display looks different from Figure 7.1, choose Edit, Change Display.

Required Entries   As a rule, unless the field has a question mark in it, it's not a required entry. However, you will see exceptions to this later in this lesson.

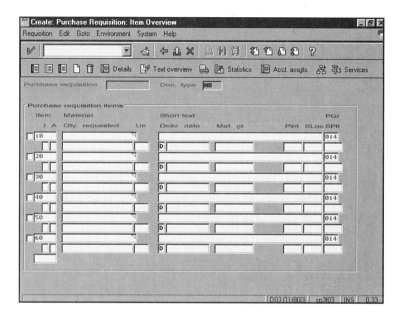

FIGURE **7.1**   When you create a purchase requisition, you must specify the items to be requested.

5. To see how SAP R/3 uses the status line to communicate, click Save. SAP R/3 displays an error message in the status bar and temporarily grays all the fields to indicate that you can't enter information in them (see Figure 7.2).

6. Press Enter to acknowledge the message and to clear the fields. (Remember that to get more detail on an error message, you can click the message.)

 Default Item Numbers   You don't need to enter the item number; it's assigned by SAP R/3. It's used to distinguish this item from others in the requisition. It may increase by ones or tens, depending on your system.

Field-Level Help   Remember that if you need more information on a particular field, you can move your cursor to it and click Field-Level Help (the question mark button) on any screen.

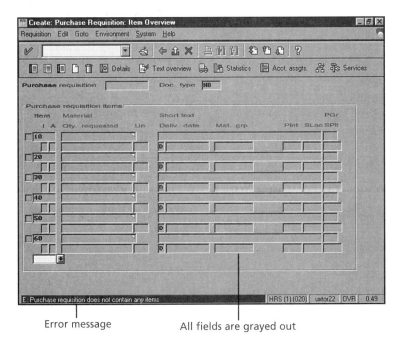

Error message   All fields are grayed out

Figure 7.2   SAP R/3's status line says that you're trying to save a requisition with no items on it.

7. Move your cursor to the first Material field and enter a valid material number for your company.

Required Entries   I said there were exceptions to the rule saying that required entry fields are shown with a question mark. The material number field is one of these, because you must supply either a material number or a description. Because you need only one or the other of these fields, they don't show the usual question mark for required entries.

8. Tab to the Plant (Plnt) field, enter the number of a plant that stocks the item, and press Enter.

SAP R/3 looks up the numbers you typed to verify that they're valid material and plant numbers. For the configuration shown in Figure 7.3, 1500-520 is the number for 10-W-30 motor oil.

Code Entries   SAP R/3 represents many items with codes (product numbers, storage locations, and so on). If you enter an invalid code, SAP R/3 displays an error message in the status bar. If the code is valid, SAP R/3 looks up the description and inserts it into the Short text field. It also fills in the appropriate Un (Unit of Measure) and Mat. Gr. (Material Group), such as CSE (case) and 010 in Figure 7.3.

9. When a valid entry is made, the cursor moves to the next empty required field. In the example shown, it is Quantity (Qty. requested). The command line asks you how much of the item you want.

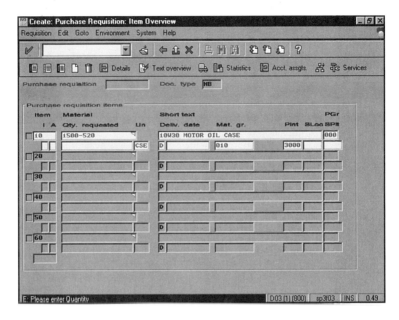

FIGURE **7.3**   You type the material number and plant; SAP R/3 looks up the rest.

LET SAP R/3 LEAD THE WAY

If you aren't sure whether you've filled in enough information to complete the record, you can let SAP R/3 guide you along. Starting where you left off in the previous exercise, work through these steps to see an example of how SAP guides you through a task:

1. Enter a purchasing group (if you haven't already) and press Enter. SAP R/3 looks at the fields and displays a message like the one in the status bar in Figure 7.3, prompting you to fill in anything missing.

2. You are asked how many or how much of the material you need. Enter a numeric value and press Enter.

3. SAP R/3 displays another "guiding" question, this time asking you to enter a delivery date (when you need the item). Enter a future delivery date.

Choose Date   SAP R/3 provides a way for you to pick the date from an onscreen calendar. Move your cursor to the date field and press F4. Double-click a date to choose it.

Date Format   In Lesson 19, "Customizing Your User ID," you learn how to specify the date format you want to use. The format that you pick doesn't affect how SAP R/3 stores the date internally; customizing the format simply affects the way the date is presented for your individual user name. (Note, however, that your company may set a standard date format for you to use in SAP R/3.)

4. Proofread your values and press Enter. SAP R/3 accepts the complete entry. As you can see in Figure 7.4, some fields for the first line item are now grayed (no further entry allowed). This tells you that the first line has been accepted. You could still go back and edit the quantity of delivery date.

The requisition is complete and you could save it now if you had nothing else to add. For this lesson, continue by adding another line item and other details.

5. Add another line item to the requisition, asking for more of the same product to be delivered on a different date. To do this, simply tab down to the second Material field and start entering the next line as you did the first.

6. Press Enter when you're done. The requisition now has two items.

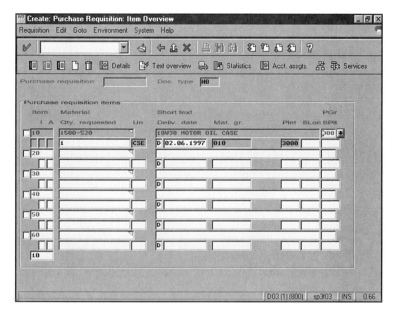

FIGURE 7.4   One line item has been accepted.

DON'T FORGET THE DETAILS

Suppose that you want to store some more detailed information related to the second line item. For example, you might want to mark the purchase requisition so that this particular material comes to your attention when it arrives. Follow these steps to add those details (or others) to the purchase requisition:

1. Click the item selection box (extreme left, empty white square) beside Item #2 on the requisition. This tells SAP R/3 that the next instruction applies only to the second line item, not the first.

2. Click the Details screen button, and the Create Purchase Requisition: Item details screen appears (see Figure 7.5). You can see by the value in the Item field (20) that this screen applies to the second line item.

Item field

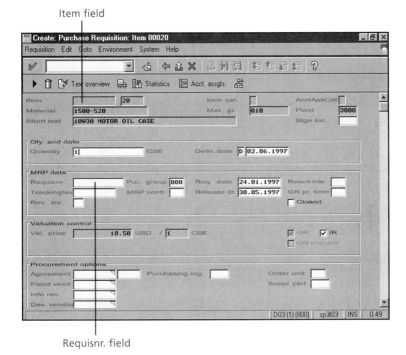

Requisnr. field

FIGURE 7.5   Use the Details screen if the Item Overview screen doesn't have the fields you need.

3. Tab down to the Requisnr. field and enter your name (so that the material will come to your attention).

4. Click the Back button to return to the Create Purchase Requisition: Item Overview screen.

5. Click Save. SAP R/3 saves the details and returns you to the initial screen, where you can enter the next requisition.

When. you save this document, SAP R/3 displays a message in the status bar informing you that a purchase requisition was created. It also creates a purchase requisition number. Write down the number your system gives you, because you will use it again in Lessons 9, "Displaying a Document," and 10, "Changing a Document."

USING DEFAULT DATA

 Shortcuts SAP R/3 is full of ways to save your work. Here is a way that works for purchase requisitions.

If you have many similar records to enter, you can use default data to simplify your task. For example, in the Create Purchase Requisition: Initial screen, you can enter data that will be the same for every item in the fields in the Default Data for Items box. So if you need to create a batch of orders for Plant 3000 and Purchasing Group 014, you can enter those values into the default data fields, as shown in Figure 7.6.

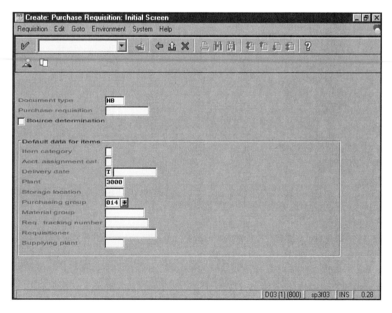

FIGURE 7.6   Using the default data fields.

When you finish filling in all the default data, press Enter; the Create Purchase Requisition: Item Overview screen reappears. For every line item on the purchase requisition, SAP R/3 has filled in the fields for which you supplied default data. All you have to do is fill in the other fields as you learned to do earlier in this lesson.

Take Advantage of SAP   Don't be afraid to press Enter if you think you're finished with a task. SAP R/3 will guide you to fill in any missing information.

In this lesson, you learned how to create a business document for which you already knew the values for the required fields. (The example you used was purchase requisition, but the principles are the same for other business documents. The key is to let SAP R/3 guide you.) In the next lesson, you see how to use matchcodes to look up values for fields.

LESSON 8

USING
MATCHCODES

In this lesson, you see how to use matchcodes to have SAP R/3 look up records for you.

USER REQUIREMENTS FOR THIS LESSON

For this lesson, you will need one of the following:

- A user logon name with authority to create a purchase requisition

- Another application area where you have authority to create a document

You will create a purchase requisition as the example. The way SAP R/3 uses matchcodes when you create this document represents how it uses them when you create (or display or change) other documents.

EXPLORING MATCHCODES

SAP R/3 uses matchcodes so you don't have to remember all the codes used for different items in your organization. You can have SAP R/3 look up items such as product numbers or purchasing groups:

 Matchcode A tool you can use to have SAP R/3 locate the field values corresponding to selected items. A good understanding of matchcodes can give you a real boost in getting the most out of SAP R/3.

- Any field that displays a small triangle in the top-right corner has a matchcode (see Figure 8.1).

- When you move your cursor to one of these fields, the down-arrow appears beside it.

This matchcode indicator appears when your cursor is in the field

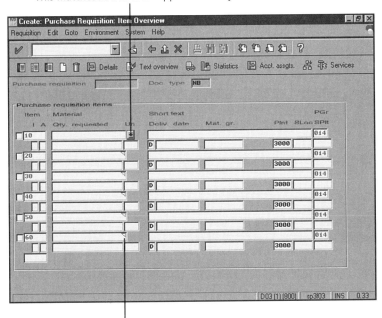

Matchcodes are available for these fields

FIGURE 8.1   Some fields have matchcodes available.

 Are There Matchcodes?   No triangle doesn't necessarily mean that there are no matchcodes. The only way to be sure is to tab to the field and press F4 (Possible Entries). SAP R/3 presents a matchcode list or tells you that they aren't available.

Work through the following exercise to learn firsthand how to use matchcodes:

1. Start from the Create Purchase Requisition: Item Overview screen. (You worked with this screen in the last lesson.)

2. Move your cursor to the Material field for one of the line items.

3. Click the down arrow beside the field or press F4, and SAP R/3 displays a Selection of Search Method dialog box (see Figure 8.2). Which matchcode ID you use depends on what you know about the material.

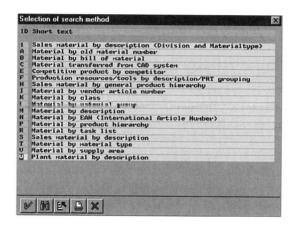

FIGURE 8.2   SAP R/3 asks which matchcode it should use.

 I Didn't Get that Window   Nothing creates more confusion among new SAP R/3 users than the multiple matchcodes available. If you didn't get the Selection of Search Method window, click the New Search button in the window that does appear.

Matchcode IDs   A system by which SAP R/3 distin-
guishes between several different matchcodes that
may be available for a field. In the example in Figure
8.2 , Matchcode ID "K" would help you find a material
number for which you know the material class.

4. Assume that you know the material description. Double-click
   matchcode W, Plant material by description, and a Restrict Value
   Range dialog box appears (see Figure 8.3).

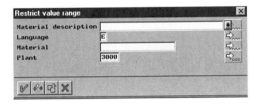

FIGURE **8.3**   A Restrict Value Range dialog box narrows the search.

 Consolidating Codes   Some companies, when they
install SAP R/3, take advantage of the opportunity to
consolidate the way products are numbered. For
example, if Marketing uses one set of numbers for a
particular product and Manufacturing uses another
set for the same product, SAP R/3 can accommodate
both sets of users until everyone understands the new
consolidated numbers. (Some earlier numbers may be
carried on in a field called "Old Material Number.")

5. You can enter information into any fields presented to narrow the
   search, and then press Enter. (For this example, just press Enter.)
   A window appears, listing the values from which you can choose
   (see Figure 8.4).

Quicker Response? The more you can narrow your search, the quicker SAP R/3 can come back with your list.

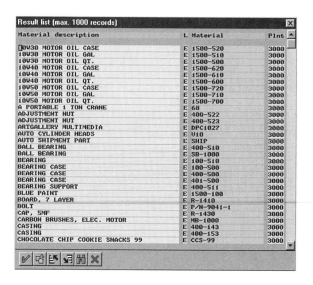

FIGURE 8.4   Choose a material number.

6. Double-click the material you want to include in your purchase requisition. SAP R/3 takes you back to the Create Purchase Requisition: Item Overview screen. Notice that the correct material code is inserted into the field.

7. Press Enter; SAP R/3 fills in the other fields. Because this product is listed on the material master, SAP R/3 "recognizes it" and supplies the appropriate short text, Unit of measure, and Material Group.

Go with the Flow If you don't know whether you've filled in all mandatory fields, press Enter; SAP R/3 will let you know if anything is incorrect or missing. (For example, it might let you know that you need to supply a purchasing group or plant.)

8. Although no arrow and no triangle are showing for Purchasing Group, a pick list is still available for it. Tab over to the field and press F4.

9. Double-click an item to select it. You are returned to the Create Purchase Requisition: Item Overview screen.

10. If you continue to press Enter, you will be prompted for the missing item's Quantity, Delivery date, and Plant. Enter a Quantity and Delivery date as you did in Lesson 7, "Creating a Document." After you complete the required fields for the line item, the cursor advances to the next line. (This is how you know you've filled in all the required fields.)

11. After you enter all the information, click the Exit tool button. If you've made changes that you haven't saved yet, SAP R/3 displays the Exit document dialog box. Click Yes to save the document and then exit; click No to discard the document and exit. (You also can click Cancel if you decide you don't really want to exit after all.)

 Dialog Box Caution   Dialog boxes like this one can prevent you from accidentally losing your work. Never let responding to them become a habit. Follow this simple proverb: "Engage brain before clicking mouse."

USING A DIFFERENT MATCHCODE

Sometimes, the Restrict Value Range dialog box doesn't list the field that you want to search with. If you need to get to the Selection of Search Methods dialog box again (to pick an alternate matchcode), click the New Search icon (see Figure 8.5).

Matchcode W is a great one to use for materials, because you can use it to show only the materials stocked at your plant. If you're seeing a lot of `Material XXXXX not stocked at plant YYYYY` messages, maybe this is the matchcode for you.

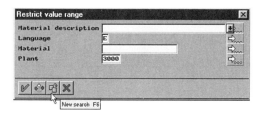

FIGURE 8.5   New Search takes you back to the Selection of Search Methods dialog box.

TEXT SEARCHING AND WILDCARDS

SAP R/3 also allows you to search text fields by using *wildcards*. For example, if you don't know a product number for the material you need but do know it was something for a motor, you could use a wildcard to find the material code (see Figure 8.6).

Wildcard   In poker, this is a card you can use to represent any card. In SAP R/3, a wildcard is a character you can use to represent any character or series of characters.

To learn how to use a wildcard, follow these steps to find the material number for an unknown material:

1. From the Selection of Search Method list for the Material field (refer to Figure 8.2), double-click M, Material by description. A Restrict Value Range dialog box appears (see Figure 8.6).

FIGURE 8.6   You use the wildcards in the Restrict Value Range dialog box.

2. For the example described earlier, you want to look for all records that contain the word MOTOR. Type *MOTOR*. (In general, type any word that corresponds to your company's list, enclosed with * wildcard characters.)

3. Press Enter. SAP R/3 displays only those materials whose descriptions contain MOTOR (see Figure 8.7). Notice that the material code you used in Lesson 7 (1500-520 for 10-W-30 motor oil) appears on the list.

4. Double-click the code to carry it back to the Create Purchase Requisition: Item Overview screen.

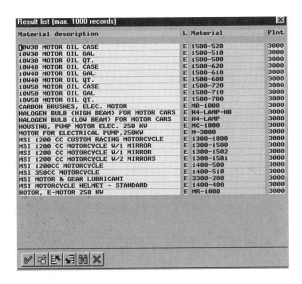

Result list (max. 1000 records)		
Material description	**L Material**	**Plnt**
10W30 MOTOR OIL CASE	E 1500-520	3000
10W30 MOTOR OIL GAL	E 1500-510	3000
10W30 MOTOR OIL QT.	E 1500-500	3000
10W40 MOTOR OIL CASE	E 1500-620	3000
10W40 MOTOR OIL GAL	E 1500-610	3000
10W40 MOTOR OIL QT.	E 1500-600	3000
10W50 MOTOR OIL CASE	E 1500-720	3000
10W50 MOTOR OIL GAL	E 1500-710	3000
10W50 MOTOR OIL QT.	E 1500-700	3000
CARBON BRUSHES, ELEC. MOTOR	E MB-1000	3000
HALOGEN BULB (HIGH BEAM) FOR MOTOR CARS	E H4-LAMP-HB	3000
HALOGEN BULB (LOW BEAM) FOR MOTOR CARS	E H4-LAMP	3000
HOUSING, PUMP MOTOR ELEC. 250 KW	E MC-1000	3000
MOTOR FOR ELECTRICAL PUMP,250KW	E M-3000	3000
MSI 1200 CC CUSTOM RACING MOTORCYCLE	E 1300-1800	3000
MSI 1200 CC MOTORCYCLE W/1 MIRROR	E 1300-1500	3000
MSI 1200 CC MOTORCYCLE W/1 MIRROR	E 1300-1502	3000
MSI 1200 CC MOTORCYCLE W/2 MIRRORS	E 1300-1501	3000
MSI 1200CC MOTORCYCLE	E 1400-500	3000
MSI 350CC MOTORCYCLE	E 1400-510	3000
MSI MOTOR & GEAR LUBRICANT	E 3300-280	3000
MSI MOTORCYCLE HELMET - STANDARD	E 1400-400	3000
ROTOR, E-MOTOR 250 KW	E MR-1000	3000

Figure 8.7   A "filtered" list.

OTHER WAYS OF SEARCHING

Although there may be many matchcodes for a single field, they all point to the same table of values. There are just different ways of searching that table. Some other ways of opening a matchcode list include the following:

- When your cursor is in the field for which you want a matchcode, press F4.

- Click the down arrow icon beside the field.

- Right-click anywhere onscreen, and then select F4 Matchcodes from the displayed list.

In this lesson, you learned how to access and use matchcodes to help you find values for fields. In the next lesson, you learn how to display a document.

LESSON 9

DISPLAYING A DOCUMENT

In this lesson, you learn how to look up and display a document directly with the document number and also by using matchcodes.

USER REQUIREMENTS FOR THIS LESSON

For this lesson, you need the number of the document you created in Lesson 8, "Using Matchcodes," and one of the following:

- A user name with authority to display Purchase Requisitions

- A user name with authority to display another business document so that you can follow along

---

Display Access Only? Sometimes a user ID is authorized to view a type of business document but isn't authorized to create or change that type of document.

DOING A DIRECT LOOKUP

Most kinds of business documents have a reference number, such as a purchase requisition or invoice number. When you know the number, you can use it directly to display the document:

1. From the Purchasing screen, choose Requisition, Display. The Display Purchase Requisition: Initial screen appears.

2. Enter the Purchase Requisition number you recorded from Lesson 7 ("Creating a Document") in the Purchase requisition field (see Figure 9.1).

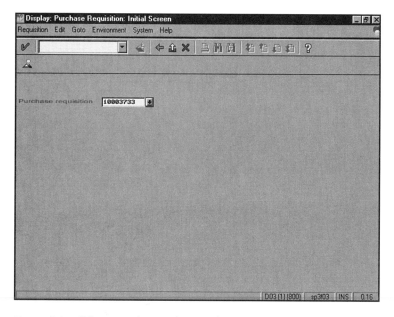

FIGURE 9.1   When you know the number, you can enter it here.

3. Press Enter. The Display Purchase Requisition: Item Overview
   screen appears. As you can see in Figure 9.2, the fields are
   grayed out (shaded). This is SAP R/3's way of telling you that
   these fields are display-only; you can't type in them. The only
   fields not shaded are the item selection boxes and the starting
   line item field (the white boxes to the left and the white box in
   the lower-left corner).

The Starting Line-Item Field   The screen normally lists
approximately the first eight line items on the document, starting with line-item 1. However, if you type
50 into this field and press Enter, your display will
start with line item 50 instead. This makes it easier to
work with long documents in which many line items
are listed, or to go to an item in a long requisition.

Selection boxes

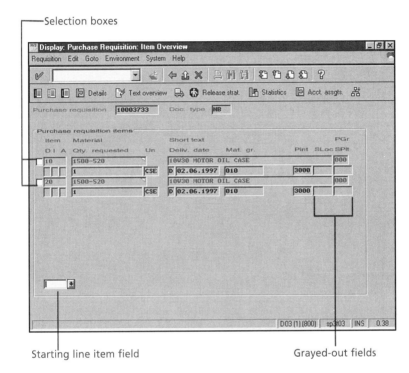

Starting line item field   Grayed-out fields

FIGURE **9.2**   Displaying the line items.

4. Click the selection box beside the second item to display
more detail, and then click the Details screen button. The
Display Purchase Requisition: Item 00020 screen appears
(see Figure 9.3).

Figure 9.3 shows the same item you saw on line 2 of the previous screen, but with more fields showing. (Notice that line item
number 20 shows in the title bar.) In this format, all the fields
are display-only.

You can see that the Requisnr. field has the value that you
entered in Lesson 7.

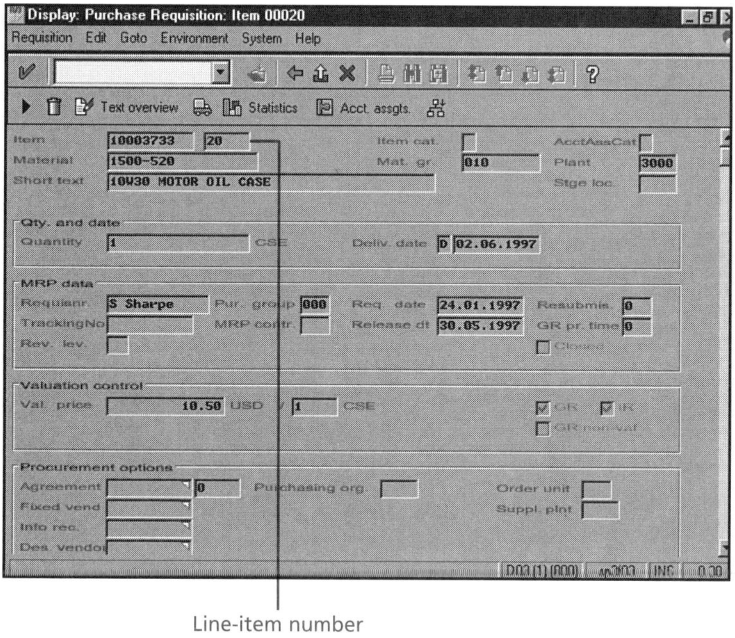

Line-item number

FIGURE 9.3   You're looking at the details for line item 20.

> **Viewing Multiple Line Items** If you want to see several line items, you can click all their selection boxes, and then browse through them in order by clicking the Details screen button and pressing Enter after each item.

5. Click the Back tool button to return to the Purchasing screen.

>
>
> **Accessing Different Screens** Different kinds of screens may be associated with every kind of document and are accessible from screen buttons. One additional screen available in the current example is the Text Overview screen. (For more details on text entry, see Lesson 14, "Editing Text.")

Additional Screens   Just because SAP R/3 provides the additional screens doesn't mean you need to use them at your company or for every kind of record.

LOOKING UP WITH MATCHCODES

Sometimes, you may not know the number of the document you want to display. You can also locate a document by using matchcodes. Follow these steps to open and display the same document with matchcodes:

1. From the Purchasing screen (where you were at the end of the previous task), choose Requisition, Display to access the Display Purchase Requisition: Initial screen (same as Figure 9.1).

2. Click the down arrow next to the field, and either a Matchcode ID dialog box or a Restrict Value Range dialog box appears (see Figure 9.4).

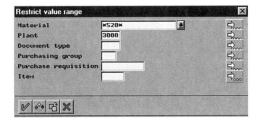

FIGURE 9.4   Enter the search values.

Wrong Dialog Box?   If the wrong Restrict Value Range dialog box appears, click the New Search button to go to the Selection of Search Methods box.

No Records? Inevitably, when you work with SAP R/3, you will sometimes select a matchcode for which there are no records. When that happens, SAP R/3 displays an error message on the status line, informing you that No Matchcode record was found. This is normal; just pick a different matchcode or take out one of your value restrictions.

3. Enter more specific search criteria (in this example, ***520*** for Material) and click Continue. SAP R/3 displays a list of the purchase requisitions that match the criteria you typed in the Restrict Value Ranges dialog box (see Figure 9.5).

 Restricting Values Is Optional   You don't *have* to type anything in this dialog box; it just produces a shorter list for you.

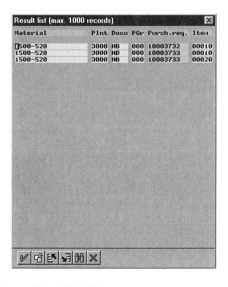

FIGURE **9.5**   Choose from this list.

4. Double-click the line containing the record you want to display, or click the line and then press Enter. You should see the Display Purchase Requisition: Initial screen with the value you selected from the matchcode list carried into the field.

5. To display the document, follow the steps for using the direct lookup method (earlier in the lesson).

In this lesson, you learned how to display a document by typing its number and by locating it with a matchcode list. You also learned that you can move between several screens associated with a document by using the screen buttons. In the next lesson, you learn how to find and change a document.

LESSON 10

CHANGING A DOCUMENT

In this lesson, you learn how to find and change a document that's already on your system.

USER REQUIREMENTS FOR THIS LESSON

For this lesson, you need the number of the document you created in Lesson 7, "Creating a Document," and one of the following:

- A user name with authority to change purchase requisitions

- A user name with authority to change another business document

FINDING THE DOCUMENT

Regardless of the kind of document you want to change, the process is similar. You bring the document onscreen, make the changes, and save it.

For the example in this lesson, you're going to work with a purchase requisition. Therefore, you begin from the main Purchasing screen again:

1. Choose Requisition, Change. The Change: Purchase Requisition: Initial screen appears.

2. Type the document number for the document you want to open, or choose it from the matchcode list as you did in Lesson 9, "Displaying a Document."

3. Press Enter. The Change: Purchase Requisition: Item Overview screen appears (see Figure 10.1).

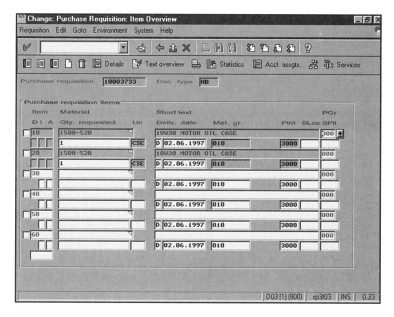

FIGURE **10.1**   You can edit the document from this screen if the field you need to change is displayed here.

    Similar Screens   The Change: Purchase Requisition screen is almost identical to the Display Purchase Requisition screen.

CHANGING A LINE ITEM

Suppose for a minute that you've just been promoted. As a result of your promotion, your job responsibilities have changed. The material you ordered in Lesson 7 should go to the attention of the unfortunate person who's taking over your old job. You need to edit the purchase requisition to reflect this change. Follow these steps to work through changing a document:

1. Click the selection box beside line item 2 to work with that item. A check appears in the box, confirming your selection.

2. Click the Details screen button. The Change: Purchase
Requisition: Item 00020 screen appears (see Figure 10.2).

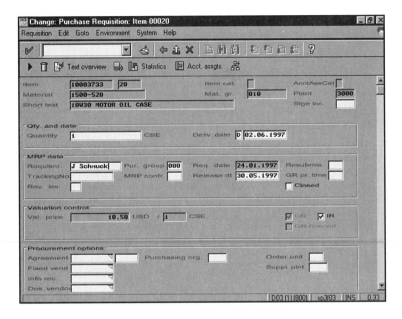

FIGURE 10.2   Change the details from here.

Check the Line Item   It's a good idea to get into the
habit of checking the line item number on the title
bar. In this case, the changes you are about to make
apply only to the second line item (which is what
you wanted).

3. Click the Requisnr. field and enter the name of the person who
is to be notified when the material arrives.

4. Click the Save button on the toolbar to save your changes. SAP
R/3 displays a confirmation message like Purchase requisition 10000014 has been changed in the status bar.

Quick Change   If you need to change an Item field that appears on the Change: Purchase Requisition: Item Overview screen (refer to Figure 10.1), you can change it directly on that screen and click the Save tool button. You need to go to the Item Detail screen (refer to Figure 10.2) only if the field you need to change isn't on the Change: Purchase Requisition: Item Overview screen.

ADDING AND DELETING LINE ITEMS

Sometimes you need to add or delete individual line items on a document. To add a line item, follow these steps:

1. Go to the Change: Purchase Requisition: Item Overview screen as you learned earlier in this lesson (refer to Figure 10.1).

2. Place your cursor in the first field of the first empty line item and begin filling in data. (In the case of the sample Purchase Requisition, it's the Material field for line item 3.)

Those Pesky Item Numbers   You can skip the Item field and just let SAP R/3 take care of the line item numbers. SAP R/3 proposes that the third line item should be (are you ready for this?) number 3. Unless you have a compelling reason to make it something else, there's no need to change it.

3. Click the Save tool button to save your requisition with the new line item added.

To delete a line item, follow these steps:

1. In the Change: Purchase Requisition: Item Overview screen (refer to Figure 10.1), click the selection box beside the line item you want to delete.

2. Choose Edit, Delete.

3. Click the Save tool button to save your purchase requisition with the line deleted.

In this lesson, you learned how to change documents that already exist on your system. In the next lesson, you learn how to use list displays.

Lesson 11

Using List Display

In this lesson, you learn how to select and display document lists.

User Requirements for This Lesson

For this lesson, you need to know the document number you created in Lesson 7, "Creating a Document," so that you can choose selection criteria that include that particular item. For the examples in this lesson, you use a purchase requisition as your sample document to display lists. It's typical of other documents you can look up on SAP R/3.

Reporting with List Display

This lesson shows you how to display a list of documents. Because you normally need to see only part of a list, it shows you how to limit the list. Some people use this to limit their list, say, to requisitions for their division only. Follow these steps:

1. From the Purchasing screen, choose Requisitions, List Display, General. The List Display of Purchase Requisitions screen appears (see Figure 11.1).

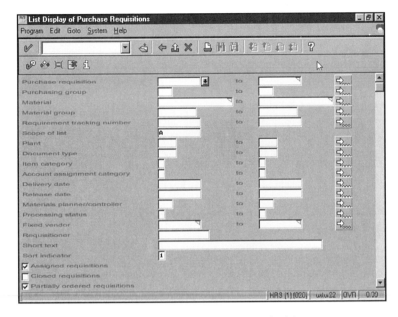

Figure 11.1 You can narrow your request with this screen.

> **Ranges** You will often want to specify a range of values on this screen. Use the left column for the starting value and the right column for the ending value. Just use the Purchase Requisition number From and To fields for now.

2. Type a range of requisition numbers here that you know contains the number of the requisition you created in Lesson 7. Then click the Execute button. SAP displays the list of purchase requisitions. Figure 11.2 shows a typical list.

> **Matchcodes** Note that some of the fields have matchcodes that you can use to look up values to insert. Some of the fields, even though they don't display the triangle, have possible entries available (Purchasing Group is one of these). You can choose to

enter values in any field combination to limit the list
display, or you can choose to display all records by not
filling in any fields.

Scroll up and down the list

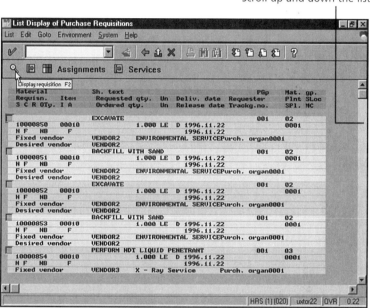

Figure 11.2   The top of the list you requested.

Stacked Fields   There are several screen lines for each
record in this list. SAP R/3 makes it easier for you to
see which fields belong to which record by shading
the lines in groups. Also, some field titles are abbreviated and are stacked as they were in Lesson 3,
"Getting Around the Screen." Again, if you are unsure
of what an abbreviated name means, click it and then
click Field-Level Help.

3. To get a better look at a requisition, click it and click the Display Requisition tool button. SAP R/3 displays a detail screen similar to the one in Figure 11.3 for the requisition you selected.

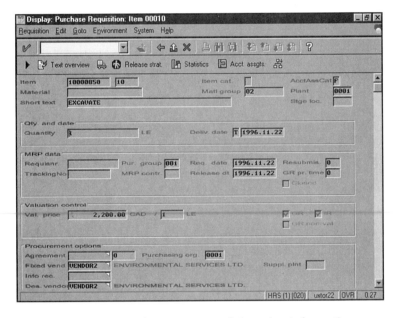

Figure 11.3 You can also get to any of the other information screens related to this requisition by clicking the appropriate tool button or selecting from the Goto menu.

4. Click the Back tool button to return to the List Display of Purchase Requisitions screen.

5. From the List Display of Purchase Requisitions screen, click a line and then click the Detail icon. SAP shows the details of the selected requisition in a screen like the one in Figure 11.4.

6. To close the dialog box, click the Close (×) button. Then click the Back tool button to return to the List Display of Purchase Requisitions screen.

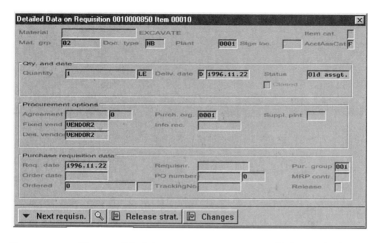

Figure 11.4   You could click Next Requisn. to scroll through the items one at a time.

MORE POWERFUL SELECTIONS

Extended selection screens allow you to limit the list display in almost any way you can imagine. Assume that you are responsible for all plants between 400 and 500, except for 404 (which is somebody else's responsibility). You could fill in **400–500** as a range, and enter **404** as a single value exclusion.

Take another look at the List Display of Purchase Requisitions screen in Figure 11.1. You can use it to do some very powerful selections:

1. Position your cursor on the Multiple Selection icon, and a Quick info box appears. Click Multiple Selection. The Multiple Selection dialog box appears (see Figure 11.5).

2. Type whatever values you need into this screen. For example, ask the system to include entries for plant 337 and for any other plant in the range of 100 to 200 (except in the range 150–160). To do so, fill in value ranges for Plant as **100–200** and **150–160**. Leaving your cursor in the 160 box, click the Options button. The Plant: Maintain Selection Options dialog box appears (see Figure 11.6). This box applies to whatever range your cursor was in when you clicked Options.

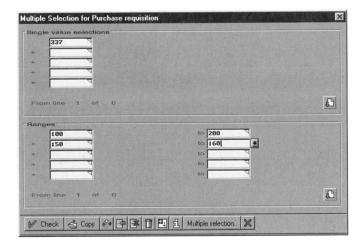

Figure 11.5   The Multiple Selection dialog box.

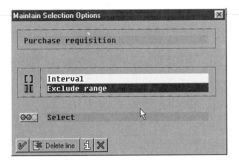

Figure 11.6   You can choose ranges to be included or excluded.

3. Select the Outside Range option to exclude the range between the specified values. With the values shown, for example, you are telling SAP R/3 to exclude values in the range of 150 to 160.

4. Click the check mark button to return to the Multiple Selection for Plant dialog box. The range you entered for exclusion appears in the Ranges section at the bottom of the dialog box, as shown in Figure 11.7.

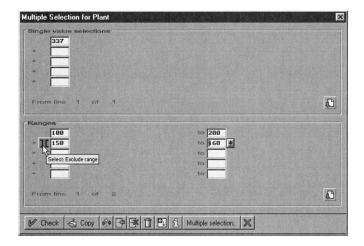

Figure 11.7   An exclusion range.

This extended selection exists throughout SAP R/3. If you are responsible for products with certain numbers, employees at a certain location, or retail outlets in a certain area, this may be the tool you need to narrow your list displays.

Saving It   You can save long or complex selections for use again later. You can also share them with other SAP R/3 users and use extended selections saved by others. See Lesson 13, "Using Variants," for more information.

In this lesson, you learned how to display lists of records. You also learned how to enter selection criteria to limit these lists. In the next lesson, you learn how to generate and print reports.

LESSON 12

GENERATING REPORTS AND PRINTING

In this lesson, you learn how to print lists and reports in SAP R/3. You also learn how SAP R/3 defines output destinations for business documents such as purchase orders, invoices, production orders, and so on.

SELECTING AND GENERATING REPORTS

For this lesson, you need a material number for which several purchase orders have been created on your system. For this example, you will use a purchase order or an item that has been approved for purchase.

> **Routing** Output is routed in two different ways: by your user ID (for lists and reports) and by predefined destination (for business documents). These predefined destinations are set up when your system is configured. With some documents (purchase orders, for example), routing can vary, with some vendors receiving faxed POs, some getting EDI POs, and others getting paper POs mailed to them.

To see how to generate reports in SAP R/3, look at an example that uses purchase requisitions:

1. From the Purchasing screen, select Purchase Order, Reporting, General Analyses. A screen similar to Figure 12.1 appears.

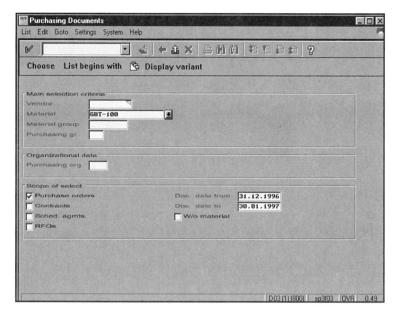

Figure 12.1   You can use this screen to limit your report in a variety of ways.

2. Supply at least one value in the Main Selection Criteria area. For now, use a material number that you know is on existing purchase requisitions. (Be sure that the date range you use is wide enough to find your document.) Then press Enter.

As you can see in Figure 12.2, SAP displays the name of your material at the top of your screen. The body of the report contains one line for every purchase order line item for the material you selected.

Data Behind Data   This list is a wolf in sheep's clothing. There's an amazing amount of detail behind it. Try double-clicking a Purch.doc number (PO number); SAP R/3 displays the original PO. Then click the Back tool button to get back to the report.

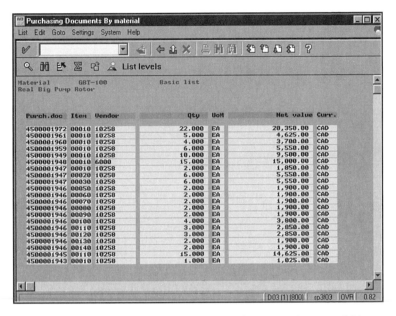

Figure 12.2   In this demo system, material GBT-100 is a "Real Big Pump Rotor."

3. Click the Sort icon to see how SAP R/3 can sort your report.
   Through the Sort dialog box (see Figure 12.3), you can do sub-
   sorts. For example, you can choose Vendor as the first sort and
   Plant as the second. This would produce a list sorted first by
   Vendor and then, within Vendor, sorted by Plant.

Figure 12.3   Experiment with different sort combinations.

4. Set your sort options and then click the check mark button. SAP rearranges the items in the list based on the sort order you selected.

5. When you are finished with sorts (but while the report lines are still onscreen), click the Total button. The Total Variants dialog box appears (see Figure 12.4).

Figure 12.4 The dialog box shows the active variant and lists the other variants for which you can total the items in the list.

6. Double-click Purchasing document totals to display a summarized list like the one in Figure 12.5.

Drilling for Data If you see a line with several items on it (look in the Number column), you can double-click that PO number to drill down to the detail behind it. When you finish, click the Back tool button to return to your report.

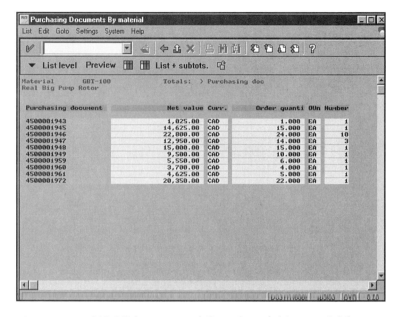

Figure 12.5   SAP R/3 has summed the value of this material for each purchase order that contains it.

7. Click the List + subtots. tool button to display the list with subtotals (see Figure 12.6).

8. Click the List level tool button to see an overview of generated list levels similar to the one in Figure 12.7. The third item on the list (item 2) is highlighted, indicating that it's the one you were on when you clicked List level.

9. Click any of the other items to recall an earlier list.

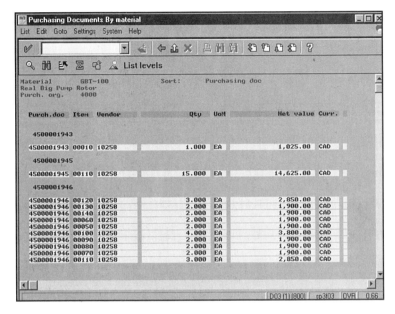

Figure 12.6   A list with subtotals.

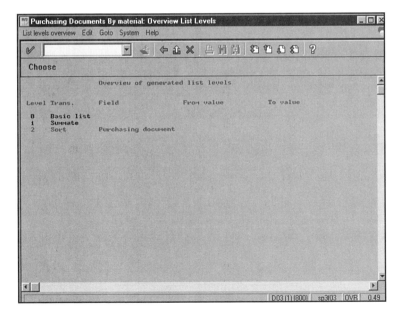

Figure 12.7   The list levels that you've generated.

OTHER REPORTS

SAP comes with many "canned" reports (along with List Display, shown in the next lesson). Many of them can be found from the first SAP R/3 screen under the menu path Systems, General report sel.

Your company will probably also have special reports developed to track key measures relevant to your business. Someone in your support organization can explain these custom reports to you.

PRINTING

With all the powerful capabilities that generating reports affords you, the need to print is almost made redundant. Do you really need all that paper? Still, sometimes you will need a hard copy of your reports. Follow these steps to print reports:

1. By following the preceding steps, set up the report you want. When the report is onscreen, choose List, Print. The Print Screen List screen appears (see Figure 12.8).

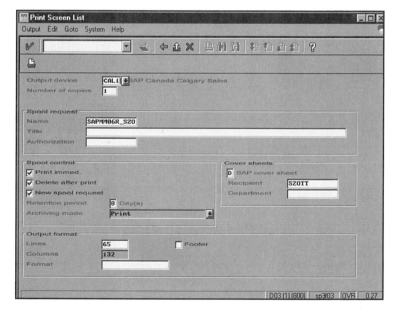

Figure 12.8   Select a printer and set printing options.

> **What About the Icon?**   On screens that show the printer icon, you can use this instead of the menu path.

2. If you know the name of your local printer, enter it here. If not, choose it from the matchcode list.

> **Where Did These Settings Come From?**   If you've assigned defaults to your user ID, those values will be carried through into some of the fields. If you don't want to use the defaults, you can go in and change the default values proposed on the Print Screen List.

3. If you select the Print Immed. option, SAP prints the report on the selected printer. If you don't select Print Immed., SAP generates a *spool request*. This request will be held by the *output controller* for printing later.

4. When you are ready to print, click the Print icon. You will get a message like Spool request (number XXXXX) created.

> **Spool Request**   A saved print job.
>
> **Output Controller**   A program that runs on the central computer to control all the spool requests.

You can access the output controller from any screen by choosing System, Services, Output Controller. From the resulting screen, you can print, change, delete, display, or check the status of spool requests.

Learning More To learn more about using the output controller, choose Help, Getting Started from Any Screen. From the Getting Started with R/3 help screen, scroll down to Printing and click it. In the box that appears, click Managing Spool Requests from the Output Controller.

In this lesson, you learned how SAP R/3 handles printing and output. You also learned that you can change its proposed settings for your user ID at the time of printing. In the next lesson, you learn how to use variants to save time when you have large or complex selection criteria for your lists and reports. You also learn how you can save and share these selection criteria with other users.

LESSON 13
USING VARIANTS

In this lesson, you see how variants save time when you have large or complex selection criteria for lists and reports. You also learn how to save and share selection criteria with other users.

WHAT YOU NEED FOR THIS LESSON

For this lesson, you need access to a report or list that has extended selection criteria available. (You learned how to specify extended selection criteria in Lesson 11, "Using List Display.")

CREATING AND SAVING VARIANTS

A variant is a saved set of selection criteria. You can use these criteria for lists and reports. You can create variants for your own use and share them with others.

Two Meanings The word *variant* has one other meaning in SAP R/3. Within Production Planning, it's used to describe products that are built with different options. For example, a Ford with an automatic transmission is a variant of a Ford with a manual transmission. That kind of variant is a separate topic and won't be covered here. If you need to know more about PP variants, choose Help, Help Library, Production Planning, Variants.

Suppose that your area of responsibility includes Purchasing groups 11, 14, 19, and 53 through 72. You might want to see requisitions for these areas only. Follow these steps:

1. From the Purchasing screen, choose Requisitions, List Display, General. The List Display of Purchase Requisitions screen appears.

2. Click the extended selection criteria arrow (beside the Purchasing Group). The Multiple Selection for Purchasing Group dialog box appears (see Figure 13.1).

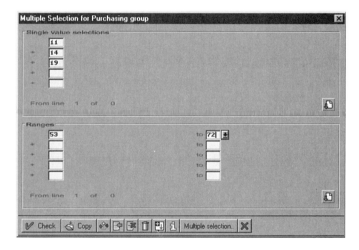

Figure 13.1 These multiple selections can get long and complex; notice the page-down symbols in both areas of the screen.

3. Fill in the boxes with the values shown in Figure 13.1 to see requisitions for your purchasing groups only. (You can use the selection criteria in a similar way for any other field.)

4. Click the Copy button to return to the List Display of Purchase Requisitions screen.

5. Choose Goto, Variants, Save As Variant (see Figure 13.2). The ABAP/4: Save as Variant screen appears. SAP R/3 prompts you for the name and description you would like to use to save your selection criteria.

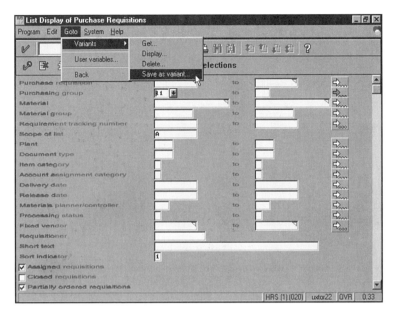

Figure 13.2 Saving a variant.

6. Enter the required information (see Figure 13.3) and press Enter. SAP R/3 displays a message that the variant you created is saved.

7. Exit the List Display of Purchase Requisitions screen by clicking the × (Cancel) tool button. From the Purchasing screen, reopen the list by choosing Requisition, List Display, General.

8. Click the Get Variant button. SAP R/3 displays a list of all variants for List Display of Purchase Requisitions to which you have access. Figure 13.4 shows only one variant on the list, the one just saved; in your case, however, there could already be more variants.

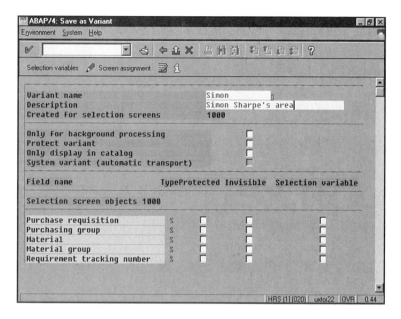

Figure 13.3   Choose a name and description for the variant.

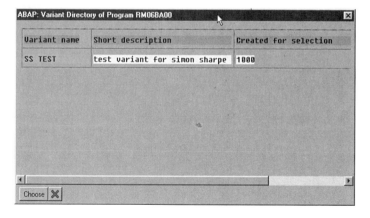

Figure 13.4   Choose a variant from the list (in this case, there's only one).

9. Double-click the variant you want to reload. You're returned to the List Display of Purchase Requisitions screen. As you can see

in Figure 13.5, the screen now contains all the criteria you keyed in and saved earlier. The colored arrow beside the second purchasing group tells you that extended selection criteria are in effect for that field.

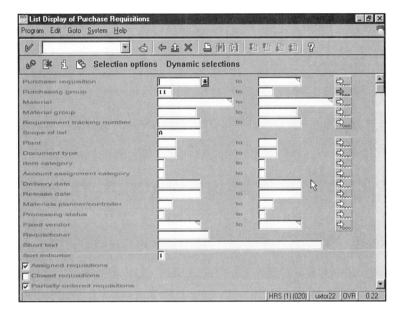

Figure 13.5   An extended selection is in effect.

You create and save variants the same way, regardless of what fields and which selection criteria you use.

The variant you just created is available to any other users on your system. They can see, use, or even change the variant you created:

- If you want to protect your variant from being changed by other users, click the Protect variant check box (refer to Figure 13.3).

- Click the Do not display variant check box if you don't want your variant to appear on the variant list (again, refer to Figure 13.3).

In this lesson, you learned how to use variants to save time when you have large or complex selection criteria for lists and reports. You also learned how you can save and share these selection criteria with other users. In the next lesson, you see how to include long text descriptions with a record and to edit that text.

LESSON 14
EDITING TEXT

In this lesson, you learn how to edit text by using SAP R/3's built-in text editor.

WHAT YOU NEED FOR THIS LESSON

You need the number of an existing requisition that you can edit.

ADDING AND EDITING TEXT

You can add text to most documents to highlight any special processing or conditions for which SAP R/3 doesn't provide fields. Some people use this in the same way they use sticky notes to draw attention to some unusual condition they need to remain aware of. To add text to a document, follow these steps:

1. On the Purchasing screen, choose Requisition, Change. Type the requisition number and press Enter. The Change: Purchase Requisition: Item Overview screen appears (see Figure 14.1).

2. Click the line item you want to attach a note to, and then click the Text Overview button to get to the text screen (see Figure 14.2). If you want to attach a short message to the requisition, enter it in this screen. (Different kinds of documents provide different numbers of types and text fields.)

3. Type your note into a field provided and click the Save tool button.

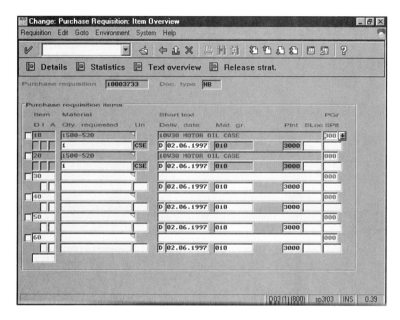

FIGURE **14.1**   You can edit requisitions from here.

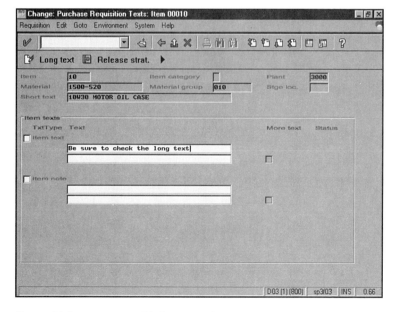

FIGURE **14.2**   You can add short text here.

4. To enter a longer passage of text associated with the record, click the Long Text button. Any short text you've already entered for this record appears on the first line of the text editor that appears (see Figure 14.3).

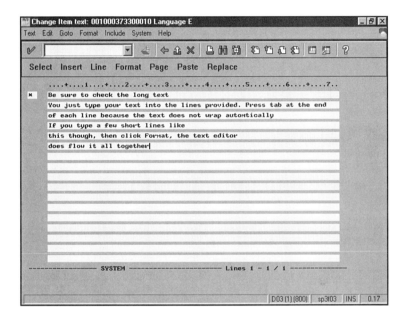

FIGURE **14.3** The short text you just entered is carried through to the first line.

Keep Your Word Processor! This text editor probably won't replace your favorite word processor, but it's useful for entering text that must be associated with SAP documents. You could spend a lot of time learning all the things it can do, but the three basics are adding text, deleting text, and inserting text.

5. Add and edit text in the text editor as follows:

- *Add text*—Enter some text (refer to Figure 14.3). You can't type past the end of the line, so press Tab when you get close to the end. Type all your text, pressing Tab as necessary to move from field to field. When you finish entering text, click the Format button to flow the text lines together.

- *Delete text*—Highlight the text you want to delete and click Delete. If necessary, click the Format button to flow the text back together.

- *Insert text*—Move your cursor to the insertion point and click Insert. SAP breaks the text to make room for the new text (see Figure 14.4). Enter your text and click End Insertion to flow the text together.

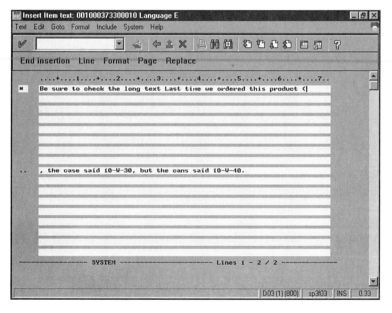

FIGURE 14.4   SAP provides empty lines for your new text.

* *Start a new paragraph*—Press Enter if you want to put text on a new line. SAP moves down to the next line, and an asterisk appears to the left of the line to show that it's a separate paragraph. Lines after the asterisk won't be flowed in with the previous lines when you click Format. However, you can delete the asterisk and click Format if you decide you want to join the lines.

It Doesn't Flow   You must move to the next line by pressing Tab (not Enter) if you want to be able to flow the lines together when you finish. You also can move to the next line by clicking it.

---

6. When you finish entering and editing the text, click the Back tool button to return to the short text screen. A check mark in the More Text box indicates that a long text message is associated with this purchase requisition (see Figure 14.5).

7. SAP displays the message Text changes were transferred at the bottom of the screen. Click the Save tool button to save your changes; the message Purchase requisition *xxxx* changed appears.

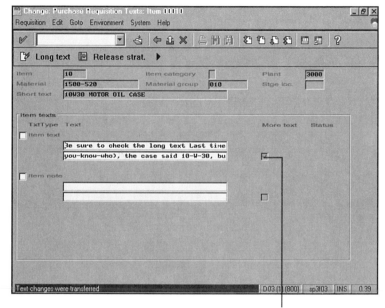

A long text message is associated with this record.

FIGURE 14.5   This is the only place that SAP tells you of the text message.

In this lesson, you learned how to add to and change short text and long text messages in business documents. In the next lesson, you learn what master data is and how to view it or change it.

LESSON 15
USING MASTER DATA

In this lesson, you learn what master data is and how to use and maintain it. You also learn what kinds of master data are available in SAP R/3.

WHAT YOU NEED FOR THIS LESSON

For this lesson, you will need one of the following:

- A user logon name with authority to change a Material Master record

- A material number and the number of a plant where it's stocked

For this example, you use a Material record as your sample master file. It's typical of other master files you create on SAP R/3. Changing other master files is similar.

KINDS OF DATA

In very general terms, there are two kinds of data in any system:

- *Transaction data* represents a system's normal day-to-day business transactions. If you couldn't create these documents, your business would stop immediately. Purchase orders, invoices, and production orders are all examples of transaction data. These are discussed in more detail in Lesson 22, "Kinds of Business Documents."

- *Master data* is relatively fixed in your system. Your company could run for days without creating new master data. Customer Master, Personnel Master, and Chart of Accounts are all examples of master data. (Note that not all master data has the word *Master* in its name.)

The authority to change master data is usually controlled more tightly than the authority to create transaction data. Although most SAP R/3 users don't need to maintain or create master data, all users must use information contained in master files in one way or another.

Maintaining Data in a Master File

Maintaining data in a master file includes adding new records, deleting old records, and changing existing records. Here is how you change a record on the Material Master:

1. From the main menu, choose Logistics, Materials Management, Material Master.

2. Choose Material, Change, Immediately. (With R/3, you also can set up a change ahead of time that will take effect on a certain date.) The Change Material: Initial Screen appears (see Figure 15.1), asking you what material you want to change.

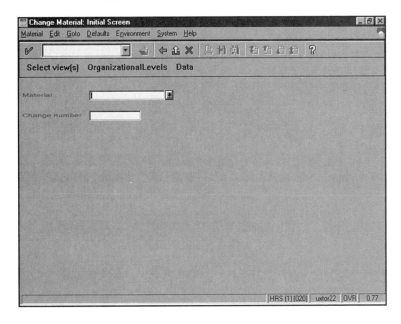

Figure 15.1   What material are you going to change?

3. You've probably guessed by now that you can key the value in directly or choose it from a matchcode list. Enter the value of a known material. The Select View(s) dialog box appears (see Figure 15.2).

FIGURE 15.2   SAP R/3 has many views available.

 Is Your List Different? Your installation may have different views available for your materials. Different materials may also have different views available.

4. You can pick one or more of these views to control which fields are displayed. This is especially useful if only one particular field is important for your job (such as "weight" to a shipping clerk or "price" to a marketing rep). For now, pick Basic Data and click the Enter tool button. After you enter the plant number, the Change Material: Basic Data screen appears (see Figure 15.3).

5. Scroll down to the Net Weight field. Type 2 and press Enter. SAP displays the message The net weight is greater than the gross weight (see Figure 15.4). This message makes sense—the net is 2, and the gross is nothing because you haven't entered one.

6. In the Gross Weight field, type 3 and press Enter. SAP displays the message Please specify relevant unit of weight.

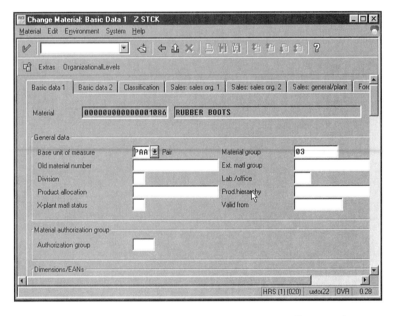

FIGURE 15.3   A material master record. Use the scrollbar on the right to scroll down.

7. Enter a unit of weight (such as KG). Or, move to the Unit of Weight field, click the down arrow to access the list of valid entries on your system, and choose an entry.

8. Press Enter to have SAP R/3 check the data checks for this screen. SAP R/3 displays the dialog box in Figure 15.5.

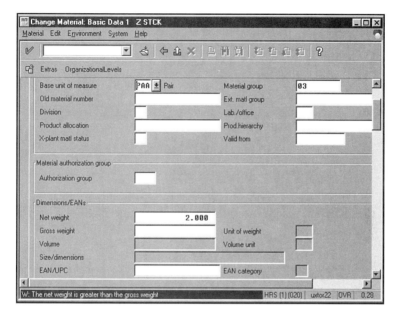

FIGURE 15.4   SAP is giving you a warning message.

9. Click Yes to save your changes. You see the message Material XXXXXXXXX changed.

FIGURE 15.5   Do you want to save your changes?

LIST OF MASTER FILES

Table 15.1 lists some common master files used by various SAP R/3 modules. Most SAP R/3 users will see only a small number of these tables in their jobs. (For a description of the various SAP R/3 modules, refer to the appendixes.) Some master files are like a table (relational), such as the Material Master. Other lists are like an org chart (hierarchical), such as the Functional Locations.

TABLE 15.1   COMMON SAP MASTER FILES

NAME	CONTENTS	R/3 MODULE
Asset Master	Managed assets	AM
Bills of Material	Components that make up a productor piece of equipment	PM, PP
Carrier Master	List of shipping companies	SD, MM
Chart of Accounts	Internal accounts to which debits and credits are charged	CO
Chart of Depreciation	Assets for which depreciation is accounted	AM
Customer Master	Customer name, address, credit terms, and so on	FI, SD, QM
Customer/Material info record	Describes material in customer's terms	SD
Equipment Master	Serial number, warranty info, and so on	PM
Functional Location Master	Locations where equipment can be installed	PM
Info-record	Vendor, product, price, vendor's part number	MM
Inspection Catalogs	General hierarchical list (attributes, possible defects, possible causes, and so on)	QM
Inspection Methods	A predefined inspection operation	QM
Inspection Plan	A defined series of inspection operations	QM
Master Inspection Characteristics	Characteristics (color, weight, and so on) that define a material's quality	QM

NAME	CONTENTS	R/3 MODULE
Material Master	Material number, characteristics, and so on	QM, SD, MM, PP
Outline Agreement	A contract to supply a variable amount of goods or services	SD, MM
Personnel Master	Name, job, salary, and so on	HR
Routings	Sequences for production	PP
Test Equipment	Equipment used for quality management	QM
User Master	Users of SAP R/3 and what they are authorized to do	All
Vendor Master	Vendor name, address, contact, and so on	QM
Work Centers	Units where work is done	QM, PP, MM

In this lesson, you learned what master data is and how to maintain it. You saw that every module uses some kind of master data and that many master files are shared between modules. In the next lesson, you learn how to use user parameters to cut down on the typing you have to do when creating new business documents.

LESSON 16

USING USER PARAMETERS

In this lesson, you learn how user parameters reduce the typing you need to do when creating new business documents.

WHAT YOU NEED FOR THIS LESSON

For this lesson, you need one of the following so you can follow along with the example:

- A user ID with authority to create a purchase requisition

- A user ID with authority to create another business document

SETTING UP THE USER PARAMETER

In SAP R/3, most fields have a short code that the system uses to distinguish it from other fields. This code is called the *PID* (parameter ID) number. To set up a user parameter for a field, you need to know its PID number.

 User Parameter   Something you set up to hold the value of a commonly used field. This doesn't affect other users—it applies only to your user ID. It also stays in effect the next time you log on.

FINDING THE PID

The following steps walk you through finding the PID for a field (Purchasing Group, in this case) so you can set up the field's user parameter.

1. In the Create: Purchase Requisition screen, move the cursor down to the Purchasing Group field. Click the Field Level Help tool button. A Help dialog box appears (see Figure 16.1).

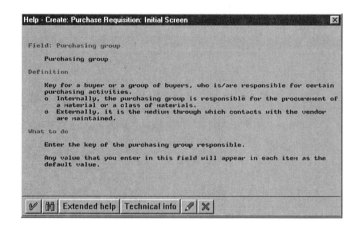

FIGURE 16.1   The first step to finding the PID number.

2. Click the Technical Info button to display the Technical Information dialog box, which contains the Parameter ID field (see Figure 16.2). In this example, it contains the value EKG. Just think of this as SAP's name for this field.

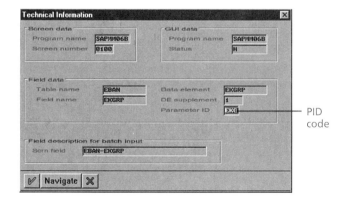

FIGURE 16.2   Finding the PID for a field.

> **Copy—Don't Type!**   You can write the information in the Technical Information dialog box (or any other dialog box, for that matter), but the cut-and-paste approach is more efficient.

3. Move your cursor to the Parameter ID field and highlight the text (press and hold the mouse button and drag over the text).

4. Press Ctrl+C (the shortcut key for the Copy command in most Windows programs). SAP copies the highlighted text to the *Clipboard*. You can't see the text in the Clipboard, but you will see that it's still there when you paste it in later.

> **Clipboard**   A temporary Windows storage area for data you want to cut or copy from one location and paste to another. You can also use it to cut and paste between other applications (such as your email) and SAP R/3.

5. Click × (Cancel) at the bottom of the dialog box to close it. Do the same for the dialog box behind it.

SETTING THE PARAMETER

Now that you know the PID for the field, you can set its default value. To better understand how this can make your work easier, consider this scenario: If 99 percent of your work is in Purchasing organization #8, you could set that as the default through the Parameter ID. As a result, this field is filled in for you automatically and, 99 percent of the time, you don't have to enter anything for it. (Of course, you can always type over the default when necessary.) To set the default value, follow these steps:

1. To get to the screen where you set the default value for the user parameters from any screen, choose System, User Profile, User Parameters. The Maintain User: Parameters screen appears. In Figure 16.3, somebody has already set up some user parameters.

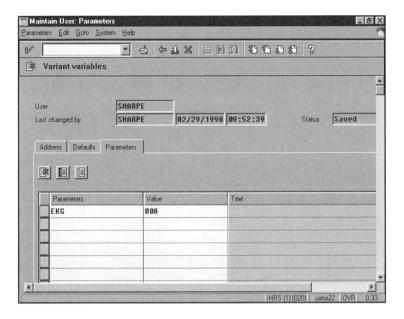

FIGURE 16.3   Add new user parameters here.

2. To tell SAP R/3 which field you're talking about, place the cursor in the PID column and press Ctrl+V to copy the parameter ID from the Clipboard.

3. In the Parameter Value column, enter the value you want to carry through into your screens. (You don't need to enter anything in the Short Text column; it's just SAP's description of the field for which you're setting up a parameter.)

 Changing Values   Don't worry about not being able to change the value later. When SAP R/3 uses a parameter ID to fill in a field, it's just giving you a starting value. You can type over that value if you want to.

4. Click the Save tool button; the status line tells you that your parameters were saved. Then click the Back tool button to return to the previous screen.

Maintaining the User Parameter You can set up as many fields as you want with default parameter values. You can also delete any of them by highlighting the line, clicking Delete Line, and then clicking the Save tool button.

If you go to the Create: Purchase Requisition screen, notice that the Purchasing Group field (see Figure 16.4) is filled in automatically with the value 008, as specified. This value is now filled in on every screen that contains this field. You can use user parameters to automatically fill in whatever fields make sense for your job. You can change or delete any of these settings at any time.

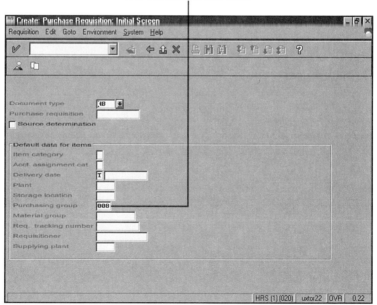

FIGURE 16.4 The value 8 is the user parameter for this field.

In this lesson, you learned how to use user parameters to cut down on the typing you need to do when creating new business documents. In the next lesson, you learn how to use user menus to provide custom access paths.

Lesson 17

Using User Menus

In this lesson, you learn how to use user menus to provide custom access paths.

What You Need for This Lesson

For this lesson, you need access to several SAP submenus so that you can set up your own access paths.

 Access Paths The sequence of menus and menu commands you need to select to get to a screen.

Setting Up a User Menu

A *user menu* enables you to set up direct access paths to those parts of the system that you use the most frequently. If most of your work is buried deep in several menu levels, a user menu will simplify your way of getting to it. Follow these steps to set up a custom menu:

1. From any screen, select System, User Profile, Start User Menu. The User Menu window appears (see Figure 17.1).

2. Place the cursor on your user ID and click the Configure button. An empty user menu appears.

3. Click the New Entries button. SAP R/3 displays a dialog box in which you are to supply a name for this menu area (see Figure 17.2).

4. Enter a name for your new area, such as **Purchasing**.

FIGURE 17.1   Starting a new user menu.

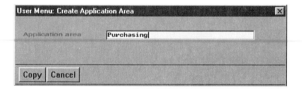

FIGURE 17.2   You can use any name that suits the way you work.

5. You have to tell SAP which standard menu choice you want to copy to your own user menu. Click the Copy button, and the structure of the standard SAP R/3 menu appears (see Figure 17.3).

6. A plus sign in front of an entry indicates subentries. Open up successive levels by clicking plus signs until you get down to the function you want to add. Select an item and click Copy. The User Menu: Change Text dialog box appears (see Figure 17.4).

7. *(Optional)* Although SAP R/3 already has a name for the menu item, you can change how it appears on your custom menu, naming it anything you want. For example, you could use the name **Create Vendor known**, as shown in Figure 17.4.

Click here to see the subentries

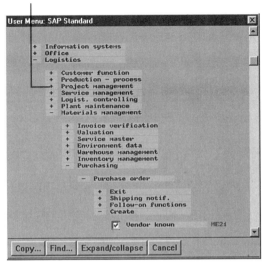

FIGURE 17.3   Click a selection box to choose an item.

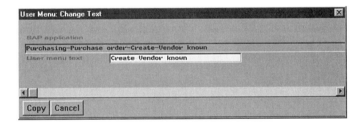

FIGURE 17.4   How do you want it to appear on your menu?

8. Click Copy. SAP R/3 adds one area (Purchasing) to your user menu, as well as one item (Create Vendor known) under it. Repeat steps 6–8 to create a structure like the one shown in Figure 17.5.

9. Click Save to save your new menu. Then click the Back tool button to return to the previous screen.

To activate your user menu, log off and then log back on again. You'll see that the User Menu window shows the names of the areas and the menu choices you specified (see Figure 17.6). To open and close branches, click the plus and minus signs; to make a selection, double-click an item.

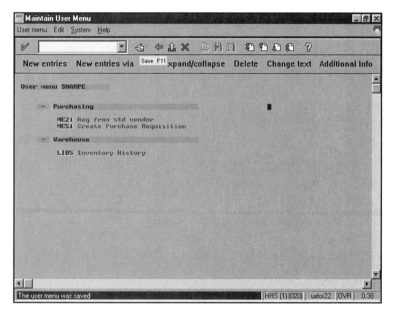

FIGURE 17.5   The structure of your new menus.

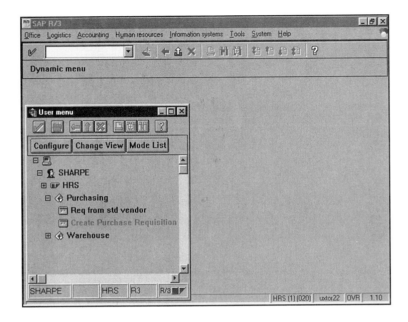

FIGURE 17.6   Your finished menu.

In this lesson, you learned how to create and use your own menus. In Lesson 18, "Using Transaction Codes," you learn how to bypass the menus completely by using transaction codes and how to run multiple sessions of SAP R/3 and move between them.

LESSON 18

USING TRANSACTION CODES

In this lesson, you learn how to bypass the menus by using transaction codes, how to look up the transaction codes for screens to which you know the menu path, and how to run multiple SAP R/3 sessions and move between them.

WHAT YOU NEED FOR THIS LESSON

For this lesson, you need one of the following so that you can follow along:

- A user ID with authority to display purchase requisitions
- A user ID with authority to display another transaction

GETTING DIRECTLY TO A TRANSACTION

Every SAP R/3 screen has a transaction code. You might find it helpful to jump right into a screen to check a value such as a price or a stock level.

 Transaction Code A shortcut that takes you directly into the SAP R/3 screen that begins a particular transaction.

Here is how you use a transaction code to go to a particular screen and find the information you need:

1. From the first SAP R/3 screen, click the command field to move your cursor there (see Figure 18.1).

Command field

FIGURE **18.1**   Enter the transaction code in the command field.

2. Type **/n** followed by the transaction code, and press Enter. For this example, type **/nme52** in the command field. (I'll explain the reason for /n later in this lesson. Note that the slash is a forward slash, not a backslash.) Because me52 is the transaction code for the Change: Purchase Requisition screen, the Change Purchase Requisition: Initial Screen appears.

Should You Use Them?   Some users find that using transaction codes rather than the menus makes moving directly to a screen convenient. Although experienced users often use transaction codes, you shouldn't use them when you're learning SAP R/3; menus are a less intimidating way to learn the system. Transaction codes are a throwback to the "old days" in computing, when you had to memorize lists of cryptic commands. The problem is, if you know how to get to a screen only by using transaction codes and then forget a code, you won't know how to find your way back to that screen.

FINDING A TRANSACTION CODE

After you're comfortable with SAP, you may find that you prefer using transaction codes to get around. But suppose that you don't know the transaction code for a screen you need to access. No problem. You can find the transaction code for any screen your system uses. Here's how:

1. Go to the screen for which you want to find the transaction code.

2. Choose System, Status. SAP displays the System: Status screen (see Figure 18.2). The transaction code is clearly labeled here— in this case, it's ME52. If you want, write down the transaction code for future reference.

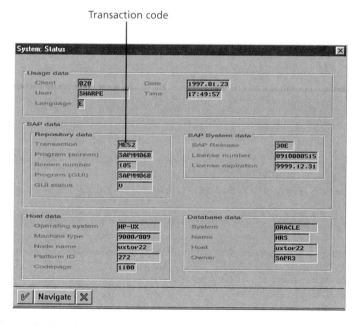

FIGURE **18.2**   The System: Status screen.

Transaction, Not Screen   The transaction code is not really specific to a *screen*, but to a *transaction*. For example, Create Purchase Requisition is a transaction that can include several screens. If several screens are required to complete a transaction, entering the code simply takes you to the first one.

USING TRANSACTION CODES TO OPEN A NEW SESSION

At the beginning of this lesson, you typed **/nme52** in the command field. But you knew that ME52 is the actual transaction code. So what does the /n prefix do? It tells SAP *how* you want it to use the transaction code. There are two ways of using a transaction code. You indicate which code you want by preceding the transaction code with /n or /o:

- /n tells SAP that you want it to abandon the screen you are currently on and move to a new screen, which is identified by this transaction code.

- /o tells SAP that you want to go to a new screen identified by the transaction code, but that you want your original *session* to remain open (so you can have two open sessions). To try this method, in the main SAP R/3 screen type **/ome52** (o as in *orange*). The same Change: Purchase Requisition: Initial screen appears on top of the previous screen (see Figure 18.3).

Session   An independent job running in its own window. You can have several sessions open at once.

Session #1   Session #2 (active)

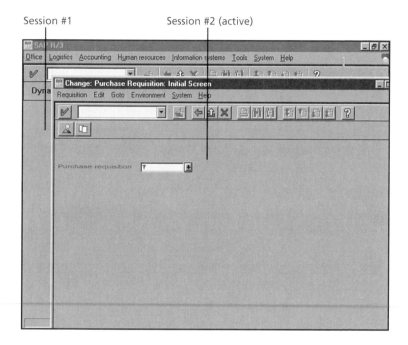

FIGURE 18.3   You can have two sessions open on the desktop at once.

Why is having more than one session open important? Sometimes when you are midway through one transaction, you need to check something in another part of the system. Suppose that you're creating a requisition and want to check something on the vendor master. If you know the transaction code for displaying the vendor master, you can open a second session while still keeping the first one open.

When you have more than one session open, you can move back and forth between them as you would between other programs and documents open in Windows 95/98.

OPENING A NEW SESSION ANOTHER WAY

Sometimes you may want to open another session, but you might not know the transaction code you need to get there. You can start another session from any screen by choosing System, Create Session. SAP opens a new session that starts at the initial SAP R/3 screen. Then you can use the menus to navigate to where you want to be.

You can close any session by clicking the Close (×) button or by repeatedly clicking the Exit tool button.

 I Can Do That from the Desktop!   Of course, you could just open another session from the Windows desktop by clicking the icon you used to launch SAP R/3 in the first place. But if you do that, you must log on again with your user ID and password. It's much easier to create a new session from within SAP R/3.

In this lesson, you learned how to find and use transaction codes. You also learned how to open and close new sessions and how to move between them. In the next lesson, you learn how to customize your user ID.

LESSON 19

CUSTOMIZING YOUR USER ID

In this lesson, you see how to change your user ID settings.

SETTING DEFAULTS

Default   A certain value that SAP R/3 uses every time it encounters a particular field, unless you specifically give it another value. You can specify what you want the default for a field to be.

The following steps walk you through setting your default user values:

1. From any screen, choose System, User Profile, Own Data, and then click User Defaults. The Maintain User: Defaults screen appears. Click the Defaults tab and use the scrollbars to move down until your screen resembles Figure 19.1.

    Note the following elements of this screen:

    • The **User** field (scrolled off the top in Figure 19.1) is just your user logon name or user ID.

    • The **Start Menu** field enables you to set up a menu for R/3 to start with when you log on. For example, if you enter **ME00** in this field, you would automatically go to the Purchasing screen every time you log on. (To see how to find codes for other screens, see Lesson 18, "Using Transaction Codes.")

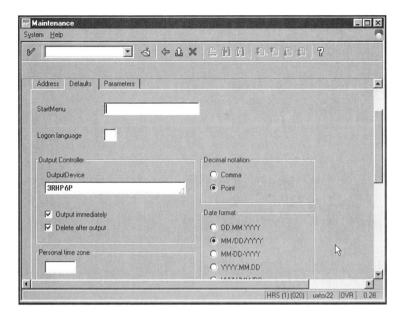

FIGURE **19.1**   Change your user defaults from this screen.

• **Output Device** is the printer that SAP R/3 will use for your reports. (To redirect your job to another printer at the time of printing, type another value over the default.) Some SAP R/3 documents may print to a predefined printer—for example, your purchase orders might always be sent to a printer in Purchasing. Changing the default here won't change the destinations for such predefined documents.

Getting Help   Remember that you can always use SAP R/3's Field-Level Help to learn more about how to use the fields.

2. Move to the Output Device field and click the matchcode corner. (If a Restrict Value Ranges box appears, click No.) SAP lists all the printers defined for the SAP R/3 system to which you are connected. Scroll through the list and find the printer you want to use. Double-click an item to select it.

3. In the Print Controller area, select Print Immediately and Delete After Printing for normal use.

4. Select the default date format that you'll use to enter dates when working in SAP and choose your preference for the decimal notation. You must enter all dates in SAP R/3 in the format you select here—otherwise, SAP won't accept your entries. Similarly, you must also use the decimal notation you indicate here.

Date Format   The format you use to enter all dates is set here. It has nothing to do with how SAP R/3 stores dates internally, just with how they're displayed and entered for *your* user ID.

5. The CATT test status control is used only for Computer Assisted Testing. Leave it as is.

6. Click Save to save your changes, and then click the Back tool button to return to the previous screen.

Keep It Simple   In practice, defining a standard date presentation for your organization is a good idea. (Somebody may have already done this where you work.) For training, it's certainly better to stick to one way of presenting and entering dates. Much unnecessary confusion is created when date formats in training materials don't match the format of a new user's ID.

CUSTOMIZING THE WINDOW AND CURSOR

Another menu is provided to change your window and cursor control. Known as the user options menu, it's tucked away in the upper-right corner and is easy to forget. If you can't remember where to find the settings for controlling a default option, check under this icon.

Follow these steps to customize your window and cursor:

1. From any SAP R/3 screen, click the icon at the right end of the menu bar to open the user options menu.

2. Choose Options from the menu. The Options dialog box appears (see Figure 19.2).

FIGURE 19.2   The Options dialog box.

3. On the General page are the following options:

   • You can turn off the toolbars or status bar, but short of mean practical jokes, I can't imagine why you would want to.

   • The Quick Info options control how quickly the little helper boxes appear when you move your cursor to an item.

   • You can specify how SAP warns you of messages. If no Messages check boxes are checked, SAP R/3 gives you error and abort messages on a discreet little line at the bottom of the screen (as you have seen so far). However, you can have them displayed as an in-your-face dialog box and have SAP R/3 beep to get your attention.

- The System Libraries option sets how parts of R/3 are used. (Your tech support people can tell you how it's usually set in your company; you probably won't ever have to change this.)

4. Use the Colors in Forms or Colors in Lists page (see Figure 19.3) to adjust your screen colors. You can change any of these settings to suit your preferences. These colors are stored with the PC and will affect any users who log on to it.

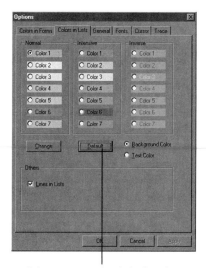

Click to restore the default colors

FIGURE 19.3   The Colors in Lists page.

For the Aesthetically Challenged   If you've changed the color settings around and don't like (or can't read) the results, you can fix them. For forms, return the Color Palettes setting to Standard. For Colors in Lists, click Default to restore the colors.

5. Explore the other options available on the Cursor, Fonts, and Trace pages. However, before you make any changes to them, write down the original settings. These pages don't provide those convenient Default buttons that return the settings to how they started.

 Screen Fonts These fonts have nothing to do with the way SAP R/3 prints information on paper; they affect only how text appears onscreen.

---

6. Click OK to close this dialog box, and SAP R/3 saves your changes.

CUSTOMIZING YOUR SCREEN SIZE

You can customize your screen size by using either of two methods: change the number of dots your Windows desktop can display, or change the default size that SAP R/3 uses for your user ID.

The first method really affects a Windows setting. Any change you make to the Windows desktop settings applies to your computer, *not* your user ID. The SAP R/3 data-entry screens were originally planned around "lowest common denominator" settings (640 dots wide by 480 dots high). With most PCs able to do better today, you will want to use a higher resolution on more and more R/3 screens.

Many PCs now can display higher resolution screens at 600×800, 768×1,024, or even higher. You can control your setting through Windows if your PC hardware supports it. You might want to go to a higher resolution for three reasons:

- For reports and lists, you can get a wider and longer viewing space, which means that you can see more items on a list. You can drag the SAP R/3 window open to a larger size.

- If your work involves having several SAP R/3 sessions open at once, you can have several overlapping 640×480 sessions open on your larger desktop.

- At 640×480, some important screen elements (like the buttons on pop-up windows) will be below the bottom of your screen.

- You can also get more line items on a document, such as a purchase order or sales order.

The downside is that the higher the resolution you use on your monitor, the smaller the text becomes.

To change your Windows setup to a higher resolution, follow these steps:

1. Choose Start, Settings, Control Panel.

2. In the Control Panel window, choose Display.

3. In the Display Properties sheet, choose the Settings tab (see Figure 19.4).

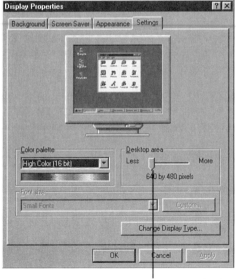

If there's room to the right of this slider, you can try a higher resolution.

Figure 19.4   Change your Windows screen settings from here.

4. Move the slider to the resolution you want. Depending on your computer, going to a higher resolution can cause the color palette to change, too. This is limited by the amount of memory on your video card.

5. Click OK to put your new settings into effect.

 Don't Be Hasty Sometimes when you change your screen resolution, it causes problems displaying the screen at the new resolution. Windows gets around this problem by changing the resolution, and then putting a message on the screen asking if you want to keep the settings. If you click Yes, you must have been able to read the message. If you don't do anything for 15 seconds, Windows thinks that you can't read the screen and changes it back. So if there's a problem, don't do anything precipitous—just sit back and wait a minute.

As I said, you can customize your screen size in two ways. The second is under SAP R/3 and applies to your user ID. To customize the default window size that SAP R/3 uses to display your screens, click the user options menu icon and select Default Size. If you have Windows set for a resolution of 640×480 (as shown in Figure 19.4), this setting will have no effect.

In this lesson, you learned how to customize the defaults and settings for your window, cursor, colors, and fonts for your user ID. You also learned that SAP R/3 can take advantage of a larger Windows desktop and how to create one on your PC. In the next lesson, you learn what configuration is and how it affects you.

LESSON 20

UNDERSTANDING CONFIGURATION

In this lesson, you learn what configuration is and how it affects you as a user.

ADAPTING TO YOUR SPECIFIC REQUIREMENTS

Most organizations have developed their own ways of conducting internal business to suit their products, services, markets, and organizational style. SAP R/3 is designed to allow each organization to adapt how the system works in the same way—to fit its own needs. *Configuration*—the process of adjusting SAP R/3 to your specifications—can make your SAP R/3 program match the way you do business.

CONFIGURATION AND CHANGE: AN INEVITABLE COMBINATION

Changing the way you do business is often a big part of the SAP R/3 equation, and the change process usually begins right away. Sometimes business methods aren't well documented within an organization; sometimes they're understood differently by different departments. Therefore, when your organization begins using SAP R/3, the first thing to do is determine and document how various departments work together.

The first aspect of configuration normally involves assembling department experts into an SAP R/3 implementation team. These experts (and some SAP R/3 consultants) document how things are done in your company. Doing a good job here is critical to the success of any SAP R/3 project.

Next, the implementation team decides whether the existing business processes should be modified. In many cases, the process of documenting and reviewing how an organization does business produces many important ideas for improvement.

The implementation of SAP in your organization gives you a chance to introduce *best practices*—ways of doing business that have evolved at some of the most successful companies in the world.

If the project team decides to make changes in addition to installing SAP R/3 (most companies do make some changes), it has the following options:

- Change the business process first and then implement SAP R/3 with the new processes

- Implement SAP R/3 with the old business process and change the process later

- Implement SAP R/3 and change the business process at the same time

Note, however, that these aren't mutually exclusive choices; companies usually choose a combination.

MOVING WITH THE CHANGES

An organization normally starts with a plain vanilla copy of SAP R/3 set up for a generic company (see Lesson 23, "SAP R/3 Industry Solutions," for exceptions). Configuration is the process of adapting this vanilla copy to your business.

SAP is working to develop more generic out-of-the-box solutions with SAP. The downside is that you need to adjust your business more to fit the product.

Given the number of complex interactions that a company experiences daily, inevitably configuration changes will need to be made up to, during, and after implementation of your SAP R/3 system.

Reactive or Proactive? In a perfect organization, all configuration changes are proactive (you see the need for changes and make them before any problems surface). In the real world, unforeseen problems necessitate reactive changes to the configuration. These difficulties are normal and usually can be dealt with quickly.

Whatever the reason behind it, configuration change is normal for any implementation. Don't be alarmed if something that works one way today works a little differently tomorrow. Here are some configuration issues that you should be aware of:

- *Don't be afraid of change*—Your SAP R/3 configuration will change most significantly before and during implementation. After that, it will continue to change when your company makes business process changes, when a new release of SAP R/3 offers a better approach for your business, and when your company is reorganized.

- *There are several kinds of changes*—A business process change could be, for example, changing the way purchase orders are approved. An organizational change might be splitting the Materials Management group across your divisions. Either move could call for configuration changes.

- *Did you find a problem?*—Don't be surprised if you discover a need for configuration changes. It's nearly impossible for the implementation team to consider all the possible variations of business processes and their interactions with the SAP R/3 program.

WHAT ABOUT THINGS SAP R/3 DOESN'T DO?

In most businesses, you can find specialized tasks that a general solution such as SAP R/3 doesn't address. When you find such tasks, you can handle it in one of two ways:

- By writing custom extensions to SAP R/3

- By using another commercially available solution and interfacing it with your SAP R/3 system

Many companies write extensions or changes to their SAP R/3 programs to accommodate unique ways of doing business. These alterations are written in a programming language known as *ABAP/4.*

 ABAP   The computer language that SAP R/3 is written in. This is normally the language your company would use for writing extensions to SAP R/3.

Although custom extensions can be helpful, there are some potential shortcomings:

- The more you write yourself, the more you start to lose the advantages of buying a software package.

- The built-in SAP R/3 Help systems won't provide any assistance on custom programs developed for your company. Your company will have to provide manuals, training, or online help for those extensions.

- The more customization that's done, the harder it is to move to new releases of SAP R/3 software.

 Specialized Systems   Most businesses need to keep some highly specialized systems, even after they implement SAP R/3. Such systems would be a refinery control system or a telephone switching system. Many companies writing these kinds of systems are working to make them easy to interface with SAP R/3. SAP R/3 doesn't aim to replace all business systems, just the core ones common to most organizations.

In this lesson, you learned what configuration is and how it affects you. You should also have learned that change is normal before, during, and after implementation. In the next lesson, you learn about SAP R/3 and the Internet.

Lesson 21

SAP R/3 AND THE INTERNET

In this lesson, you learn how SAP R/3 facilitates business on the Internet. You also look at SAP's home page on the World Wide Web.

DOING BUSINESS ON THE WEB WITH SAP R/3

SAP has developed ways R/3 (and even its predecessor, R/2) can be used with the Internet. Version 4.*x* is Java enabled.

> Java   A programming language. Think of it as an extension to your Web browser (Netscape or Internet Explorer). With Java, small programs are sent to you that automatically run inside your browser. Programs written in Java run on any browser that supports it, whether or not the browser is running on a Windows PC, a Macintosh, or a network computer.

With Microsoft, SAP has developed technologies that create numerous opportunities:

- Running the regular SAP-GUI on your PC, with connection being provided through the Internet.

- Connecting a remote user to a central R/3 system through a Web browser. The Java programs that present the SAP R/3 front end run inside your browser. Your SAP R/3 screens are displayed in Netscape or Internet Explorer. This will make it easier to distribute SAP R/3 geographically where no traditional LANs or WANs are in place.

LAN and WAN   Local area network and wide area network, the kinds of networks used by most businesses to connect their in-house desktop computers.

- Communicating ALE (Application Link Enabling) messages through the Internet.

ALE   Defines standards for coupling SAP R/3 components running in different locations. It's used for things such as consolidating sales data from independent SAP R/3 systems and updating master files on remote systems. ALE messages can be sent within SAP or from SAP to other products.

- Providing a customer ordering/payment interface. It will be possible, through specially designed interfaces, for customers to create their orders directly on your SAP R/3 system via the Internet. The necessary controls will, of course, be available.

- Providing a customer quotation/information interface. Customers can get product and pricing information through the Internet.

- Providing defined outside access to R/3 applications. You can give your customers immediate access to information regarding their orders, accounts, deliveries, and so on.

- Moving data entry out to the point of capture (the place where the information is created). Suppose that you run a network of retail outlets. You could have the managers directly input the "closing data" every night rather than send in forms. (You could set up special interfaces to SAP R/3 for these employees, so all they would need to know is the point-and-click stuff, not the whole SAP R/3 interface.)

VISITING SAP'S HOME PAGE ON THE WORLD WIDE WEB

The Internet is one area where SAP is moving very quickly. To see what SAP has developed or is planning this month, check out the company's home page on the Net.

If you have access to a World Wide Web browser (such as Netscape or Microsoft Internet Explorer), you can visit SAP on its index page at http://www.sap.com/. The SAP home page (see Figure 21.1) is a great source of information about what's new with SAP. Newsletters, technical articles, press releases, and other useful information can all be found there.

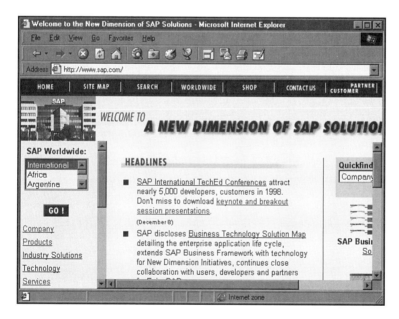

FIGURE 21.1   SAP's home page as it appeared in December 1998.

 URL (Uniform Resource Locator)   The "address" of a Web page. Every page on the World Wide Web has its own URL.

It's Not the Same! If the page on your screen doesn't look like this one, don't worry—you're still in the right place. The appearance of the SAP page varies from month to month. (Its URL stays the same, though.)

Most of the documents available for download from the SAP page are in Adobe Acrobat format. The *extension* (the last three characters of the file-name) for files in this format is .pdf. Like a magazine, this format is great for printing mixed text and graphics, but the files are usually rather large and take a few minutes to download. To read the .pdf files, you need to download the Adobe Acrobat reader from the Web; you can find it at `http://www.adobe.com/acrobat/`.

If you decide to print these documents after you download them, note that it can take a long time and (temporarily) use up loads of disk space during printing. On the other hand, browsing them onscreen with the Adobe Acrobat reader is quick and fairly easy. The SAP home page suggests a way that you can download all the PDFs from an issue of its magazine into a directory where you can read it as a single online magazine.

READING THE NEWSGROUP

Usenet is like a huge discussion group broken down into thousands of areas called *newsgroups*. You can find a newsgroup on every topic imaginable, from home brewing to astronomy—and among them is a newsgroup for SAP R/3. People post messages every day to share thoughts, ideas, and questions about SAP R/3 with other interested parties.

If you have a newsreader and your Internet service provider includes a news server, you can read or subscribe to an SAP R/3 newsgroup. Figure 21.2 shows WinVN, an example of a dedicated newsreader. Netscape Navigator and Outlook Express also contain newsreaders with which you can read newsgroups.

The newsgroup name is `de.alt.comp.sap-r3`. The `de` (for *Deutsch*) is used because SAP is a German company. Most `de` newsgroups are in German; however, most of the news in this particular group is in English.

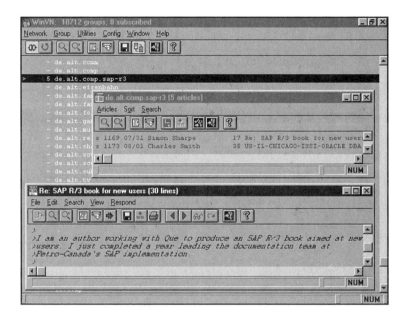

FIGURE 21.2   Cruising the SAP R/3 newsgroup with WinVN.

This newsgroup isn't sponsored or officially supported by SAP. It's just an open forum for people involved in setting up and using SAP R/3. As you'll see, many postings seem to be posted by people looking for work or companies looking for people. There's also some technical and organizational information. As in any newsgroup, you can post your own observations or questions here, if you want.

In this lesson, you learned how SAP R/3 can facilitate business on the Internet. You also learned about the SAP home page and the Usenet newsgroup. In the next lesson, you learn about the different kinds of SAP R/3 business documents and how they're used.

LESSON 22

KINDS OF BUSINESS DOCUMENTS

In this lesson, you learn the purpose of some common types of documents used in SAP R/3.

KINDS OF BUSINESS DOCUMENTS

In very general terms, there are two kinds of data in any system:

- *Master data*—This data is relatively fixed in your system. Your company could continue to run for days without creating new master data. Not all master data has the word *master* in its name. Customer Master, Personnel Master, and Chart of Accounts are all examples of master data. (These are discussed in more detail in Lesson 15, "Using Master Data.")

- *Transaction data*—This data is made up of the normal day-to-day business transactions in a system. If you couldn't create these documents, your business would come to a stop. Purchase orders, invoices, and production orders are all examples of transaction data. With *transaction data*, there's usually a chain of documents involved in any process. For example, a document may start as an inquiry from a customer, be converted into a quotation, and then work its way through the system to finally become an invoice and a payment.

It's important to know where the documents you work with come from and go to so that you understand the implications of any errors or problems that might be found in the document. Table 22.1 lists the common SAP R/3 documents and their purpose, as well as the R/3 modules that use the information, its predecessor, and some subsequent documents.

Information in each document may have been copied in from a predecessor document, or may have information carried forward into a subsequent document.

This List Isn't Definitive Many documents and relationships in SAP R/3 aren't included in this list. SAP R/3's Business Object Repository lists more than 170 different kinds of business objects. (A purchase order is an example of a business object.) Although this list isn't comprehensive, it covers the most common objects.

TABLE 22.1 **THE MOST COMMON SAP R/3 DOCUMENTS**

NAME	DESCRIPTION	USED BY	PREDECESSOR	SUBSEQUENT
Bill of Materials	Lists items needed to build a product	PP, PM, MM		
Credit Memo	Tells customers their account is credited	SD, FI		
Customer Payment	Records receipt of payment from customer	FI	Invoice	
Debit Memo	Tells customers their account is debited	SD, FI	Invoice	
Delivery	Records delivery of goods	SD, MM	Sales Order	
Delivery, free of charge	Records delivery of samples or items for complaint resolution	SD, MM	Inquiry	

continues

TABLE 22.1   CONTINUED

NAME	DESCRIPTION	USED BY	PREDECESSOR	SUBSEQUENT
Goods Issue	Authorizes goods removed from stock	MM, PP, SD, PM		
Goods Receipt	Records receipt of goods from external supplier	MM, FI, QM	Purchase Order	
Inquiries	Customer request for information	SD		Quotation
Inspection Lot	Request for inspection	QM		
Invoice (1)	Request for payment sent to customer	SD, FI	Sales Order	
Invoice (2)	Request for payment received from a vendor	FI	Purchase Order	
Maintenance Notification	Request for maintenance	PM		
Maintenance Order	Order authorizing service	PM, MM, CO	Maintenance Notification	
Material Reservation	Reserves a material that is in stock	PP, SD, PM		
Order Proposal	Proposed order for your stock or production	MM (MRP)		
Outline Agreement (1)	Documents terms agreed with customer for use over a specified time period	SD, MM		Release Order (theirs)

NAME	DESCRIPTION	USED BY	PREDECESSOR	SUBSEQUENT
Outline Agreement (2)	Documents terms agreed with vendor for use over a specified time period	MM		Release Order (yours)
Picking List	List of materials to be removed from stock	MM		
Pricing and Condition	Prices, discounts, surcharges, and so on	SD		Sales Orders
Production Order	Schedule of production of goods	PP, QM	Sales Order, Planned Order, Production Proposal	Delivery
Planned Order	Production slot reserved to fill a customer's order	MM (MRP)	Sales Order	Purchase Requisition
Purchase Order	Order for goods or services from a vendor	MM, FI, QM	Purchase Requisition	Goods Receipt
Purchase Requisition	Request to MM from business unit for goods or services	MM	Plan Order	Purchase Order
Q-Info Record	Vendor's status (blocked, allowed) for a material	QM	Quality Assurance Agreement	
Quality Assurance Agreement	Agreement with vendor that allows procurement of a given material	QM		Q-Info Record

continues

TABLE 22.1   CONTINUED

NAME	DESCRIPTION	USED BY	PREDECESSOR	SUBSEQUENT
Quotation (1)	Vendor's offer to supply goods and materials at specified terms	SD	RFQ	Purchase Order
Quotation (2) Order	Your offer to supply goods and materials at specified terms	SD	Inquiry	Sales
Release Order	Used with outline agreement to request product	MM	Outline Agreement	
Return	Records customer number, date, reason, and so on	SD	Delivery	
RFQ	Records product amount, vendor, and so on	MM		Purchase Order
Sales Order	Records customer number, date, line items	SD, MM, FI	Quotation	Delivery, Invoice
Time Tickets	Shop floor paper for worker to fill in the time an operation took	PP, FI, HR, PM		

Each kind of document has variations in how it can be created or processed. For example, a purchase order can be created from scratch, from a requisition, from the MRP process, and so on.

In this lesson, you learned about the most common documents, that documents are often shared between SAP R/3 modules, and that most documents either trigger subsequent documents or are triggered by earlier documents. In the next lesson, you learn what the industry solutions are and how they may affect you.

LESSON 23

SAP R/3 INDUSTRY SOLUTIONS

In this lesson, you learn what the Industry Solutions are and how they may affect you.

WHAT IS AN INDUSTRY SOLUTION?

A generic copy of SAP R/3 provides a starting point for most businesses. However, some companies (because of the nature of their business) can benefit from starting with a version of SAP R/3 that has been customized for their industry. Such versions are called *Industry Solutions*.

Industry Solutions versions of SAP are different from the vanilla SAP R/3 because they are (somewhat) preconfigured and have *extensions*. This doesn't mean that your company can bypass the configuration step, but it does mean a better fit between your "out-of-the-box" system and your needs. In essence, Industry Solutions give you the benefit of the learning and experience from earlier SAP R/3 installations in your industry.

 Extension An addition to SAP R/3 that doesn't come with the plain version; a program written to add industry-specific functionality to R/3.

EXAMPLES OF INDUSTRY SOLUTIONS

In the two years between the first and second edition of this book, the number of Industry Solutions has gone from seven to 20. It's safe to assume that new Industry Solutions will continue to be developed. The Industry Solutions available now include the following:

SAP Aerospace and Defense	SAP Automotive
SAP Banking	SAP Chemicals
SAP Consumer Products	SAP Engineering and Construction
SAP Healthcare	SAP High Tech
SAP Insurance	SAP Media
SAP Mil Products	SAP Oil and Gas
SAP Pharmaceuticals	SAP Public Sector
SAP Real Estate	SAP Retail
SAP Service Provider	SAP Telecommunications
SAP Transportation	SAP Utilities

HOW INDUSTRY SOLUTIONS AFFECT YOU

If you start from an Industry Solution, your configuration time will probably be shorter, and configuration will present fewer risks than if you were to start with generic SAP R/3. You also might need to adapt your business processes less than you would with a generic version.

Some kinds of industries don't yet have Industry Solutions. It's possible that your business will first implement SAP R/3 by using a generic version that has been configured for your company, and later switch to an Industry Solution–based system. This would likely be another large project, similar to (but hopefully easier than) your original SAP R/3 implementation.

INDUSTRY SOLUTIONS AND THE FUTURE

As SAP R/3 continues to develop, more than likely more Industry Solutions will become available. These solutions should become more detailed and better tuned to their respective industries as people work with them and see opportunities for increased efficiency.

Here's a glimpse of what the future might hold for SAP R/3:

- SAP is planning to decouple SAP R/3 so that companies can buy and implement only the modules they need.

- SAP R/3 is being marketed to medium-sized businesses, in addition to the large corporations using it now. Although this integration will cost them money up front, it will help not only their internal integration, but potentially also their integration with other companies using SAP R/3.

- Because of SAP R/3's integration capabilities, more companies will be willing to outsource services (by using SAP R/3 to integrate the functions) that they might not consider outsourceable today.

 Outsource   The current euphemism for contacting services to farm out functions that were formerly done by in-house staff.

The primary benefit of SAP R/3 is its integration between modules. Some people feel the Internet performs (or will perform) this function just as well and don't see a need to implement SAP R/3. Although it's true that the Net can help you get more life out of your existing systems, R/3 offers much more to business process integration than just the capability to send data between systems.

In this lesson, you learned about Industry Solutions and how they could affect you. You also learned about some future possibilities involving SAP R/3 and Industry Solutions. In the next lesson, you learn about the company-specific help that is usually provided to document how to use SAP where you work. You also learn about training and SAP.

Lesson 24
Where to Go from Here

In this lesson, you learn what other kinds of help can be provided as part of an SAP R/3 implementation.

Haven't We Had Enough Help Already?

Because SAP R/3 is designed to work in many different kinds and sizes of organizations, its help is necessarily generic. There will be procedures that you never need to follow where you work, and fields you never need to fill in (or always fill with the same value).

It therefore falls to your project team to provide detailed, step-by-step help (Task Sheets) on how to perform each business process in SAP R/3 where you work. These instructions also help define a consistent way of doing business. An example of a Task Sheet might be Create Purchase Requisition.

There are many different approaches and delivery methods for getting this help to the people who need it, but some of the common elements are as follows:

- When to follow the procedure and what needs to have occurred beforehand.

- What values are needed to complete the transaction.

- The name of each field that must be filled in and how they are used. Some approaches don't even mention fields that aren't required.

- The method for moving through the screens required for the transactions.

- The screen titles the user will see throughout the process.

- The expected end result of the procedure.

SAP itself markets two tools to help with the training process: the Personal Navigator and InfoDB.

PERSONAL NAVIGATOR

Personal Navigator is a slick tool that you can use to demonstrate a process, practice on your training system, or actually use to coach an employee through completing a transaction on your live system. Arrows appear onscreen, pointing to the next element you need to fill in (or click). Little boxes appear, telling you what to put in each field.

It is worth remembering, however, that

- Somebody on your project team will still have to go through all the steps to describe how to use SAP R/3 in your shop.

- Your users need to learn how to use Personal Navigator itself before it can help them to do anything.

- Some users still prefer to have their help on paper in addition to onscreen.

- Personal Navigator comes at a significant cost; you need to work to ensure that you get full value out of it.

InfoDB

InfoDB evolved to gather all of SAP's training materials together and provide tools for the following:

- Reuse of existing training objects (slides, exercises, and so on)

- Presentation and distribution of training materials

SAP used this product internally, and then started marketing it to clients to assist with the development of training materials.

Courses have been repackaged to more closely match job functions (such as warehouse clerk) rather than grouped into SAP modules (such as MM). Early user interfaces are improved, and SAP now sees this product as the answer for warehousing all its clients' non-relational (not in table format) information.

GET IT ONLINE

Probably the best format for these Task Sheets is as a Web page on your company's *intranet* (internal Internet). If this is done properly, the materials can be printed off for inclusion in paper training manuals and available online for later reference and distribution. It can even be plugged in to SAP's help menus.

PRACTICAL ADVICE FOR TRAINING AND GETTING TRAINED

There are many approaches to training (and learning SAP R/3). Here are some things learned from other projects:

- Slides and conceptual overviews are often overused. If you're spending more than 25 percent of your training time on concepts and overheads, you're spending too much time on it.

- Get hands-on training. The more time you spend with your hands on the keyboard, the more you will learn.

- Ask questions. The instructor should know more about SAP than you do, but you know more about your job. Ask about the exceptions. Think of problems that have happened in the past. A good instructor may not be able to answer all of these off the top of his head, but he can take them back to the project team.

- Have access to a practice system. Nothing evaporates as quickly as training that you have no chance to use.

Sharpe's Law   Unapplied training has a half life of about five working days. If you don't use it within a week, you lose half of it. Within two weeks, you lose three quarters of it. Within three weeks, some of the words sound vaguely familiar.

IT'S IN YOUR HANDS NOW

After all the consultants have left for another project (probably along with some of your long-time staff people), you will be left with the system and the knowledge to continue doing your job with SAP R/3. Don't stop there, though—nobody knows your job as well as you do. As you work with the tool and become more comfortable with it, you no doubt will discover new shortcuts or ways of extracting information that nobody on the project team foresaw.

You can combine your knowledge of your job with your new knowledge of SAP to develop better ways of doing your work.

In this lesson, you learned about the company-specific help that is usually provided to document how to use SAP where you work. You also learned about training and SAP. In the appendixes, you get a small taste of what's in the various SAP R/3 modules, as well as an idea of how the modules work together.

APPENDIX A

SALES AND DISTRIBUTION, MATERIALS MANAGEMENT, AND PRODUCTION PLANNING MODULES

 Wait! Before you read this appendix, be sure that you're familiar with the different kinds of SAP R/3 business documents explained in Lesson 22.

SALES AND DISTRIBUTION

Sales and Distribution (SD) includes the business processes used to sell and deliver products and services to customers and business partners. Information about the products and customers (both of which are stored as master data) is used in SD.

To handle these business processes, your company's structure needs to be represented in SAP R/3. For example, if you have a head office and several sales organizations (classed by region or by product, for example), the head office could be represented with a client code, and the sales organizations could be indicated by company codes. Your sales organizations could be broken down further into distribution channels. You might also have a *matrix organization* in which different divisions exist for different products. Finally, you could have sales areas where the matrixes cross. Figure A.1 illustrates this type of structure.

Matrix Organization   Exists when a subgroup in a company belongs to more than one group.

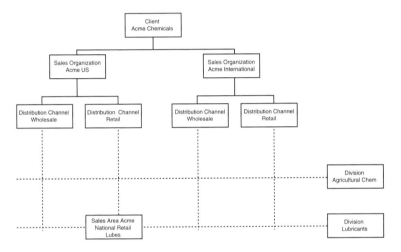

FIGURE **A.1**   One way a complex sales organization can be represented for SD in SAP R/3.

Divisions   Your organization might not use all these divisions or might use them a little differently. The structure of your company needs to be accurately rep-

To get a flavor for SD, follow a typical sale through the system (see Figure A.2). You could process a sale in many other ways.

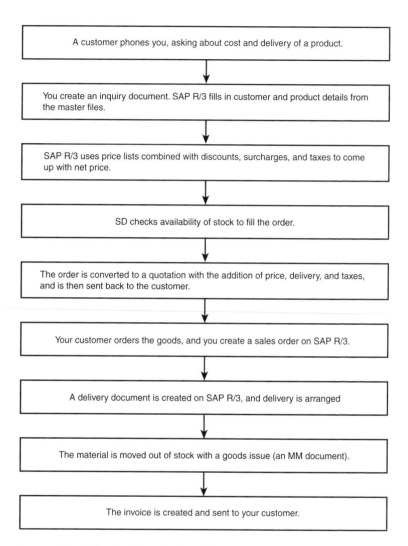

FIGURE A.2   A typical flow in the Sales process.

The following list outlines functions and benefits of SAP R/3's SD module:

- SD adapts to various scenarios. A customer might simply call and place an order, or there might be an existing contract or scheduling agreement with a customer that predefines price and delivery.

- You can price orders manually.

- SD provides for the processing of exceptions such as returns and free deliveries.

- You can create a sales order with reference to a quotation. All the appropriate values from the quotation will be copied into the sales order.

The main documents used in SD include the sales order, inquiry, quotation, outline agreement (contract and scheduling), return, no charge delivery, delivery, debit memo, credit memo, billing document, and *info record*. The main master files used by SD are Customer Master, Material Master, and Inventory Master.

 Info Record   Combines customer and product information. It lists things specific to a certain product for a certain customer. For example, you could use an info record to track your customer's product number.

SD reports the quantities to MM to ensure that stock is reserved or ordered. SD also forwards billing information to FI for credit checks and receivables postings.

MATERIALS MANAGEMENT

Materials Management (MM) includes the business processes used for purchasing, material requirement planning, goods receipt, and inventory management. Materials Management has a strong connection with SD— for instance, your company's MM department will be dealing with other companies' SD departments and vice versa.

Your company's structure also needs to be represented in SAP R/3 for MM. Figure A.3 shows a typical way you might represent your purchasing organization.

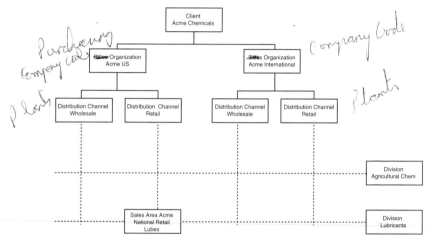

FIGURE A.3   One way a complex purchasing structure could be represented in SAP R/3.

As with SD, the top level is Client, which is normally used to represent your head office. Within Client, your organization can be subdivided into Company Code and then Purchasing Group. Purchasing Group is sometimes used to identify individual purchasing agents. You can use a matrix if you have central groups responsible for the purchase of a certain class of materials. Again, your company might not need to use all these divisions or might use them differently.

The flow chart in Figure A.4 shows a typical sequence for buying, assembling, and selling as an example of how MM works.

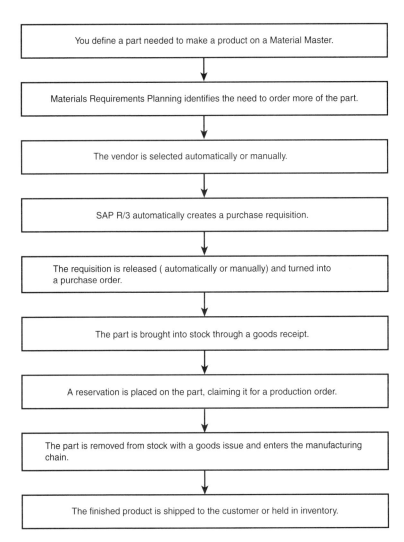

FIGURE A.4   A typical flow in Materials Management.

Availability Just because you see an item on the shelf doesn't mean it's available. It could have a material reservation against it. If you really want to know what's available, check SAP R/3, not the shelf.

MRP-Materials Requirements Planning can generate proposed orders based on order point, order quantity, Sales Orders from SD, reservations on existing stock, and so on.

The main documents used in MM are purchase requisitions, purchase orders, goods transfers, goods receipts, and goods issues. The main master files used in MM are Material Master, Inventory Master, and Vendor Master.

Purchasing passes information to Controlling (CO) so that CO can assign costs to the appropriate cost center. Purchasing shares the Vendor Master with Financial Accounting (FI). Purchasing takes information from SD to perform Material Requirements Planning.

PRODUCTION PLANNING

Production Planning (PP) includes the business processes used to plan and track the cost of production orders. The company structure reflected in PP starts at the top with Client Number, which represents your head office. The Company Code is next, followed by the units, which are subdivided into Plants and Work Centers (see Figure A.5).

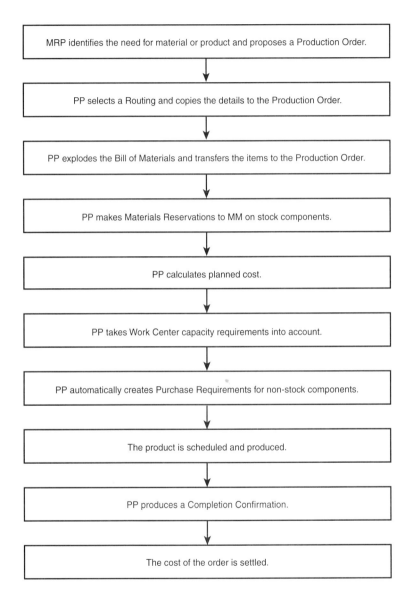

FIGURE A.5 One way of representing a production organization in SAP R/3. Part of a *Routing* is shown.

Bill of Materials (BOM), Routing   Making an analogy to a recipe, the Bill of Materials is the ingredients list, and the Routing is the instructions.

To get a quick overview of Production Planning, follow the sample production run shown in Figure A.6.

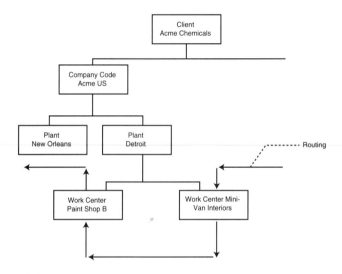

FIGURE A.6   A typical flow in Production Planning.

PP also handles the following functions:

- Scheduling of Production Resources & Tools and Capacity Leveling

- Make-to-Order (job-shop) and Repetitive Manufacturing (make-for-stock) jobs

- External processing, where your product receives some processing at an outside company

- Directing the printing of shop floor notices to the appropriate shop-floor printer

The main documents used in PP include Production Order, Bill of Material, Material Provision List, Goods Reservation, Completion Confirmation, Time Ticket, Production Resource & Tools Overviews, and Withdrawal Slip. The main master files used in PP include Routings, Work Centers, and Material Master.

PP interfaces with MM, Human Resources (HR), and CO.

APPENDIX B

QUALITY MANAGEMENT, PLANT MAINTENANCE, AND HUMAN RESOURCES MODULES

Wait! Before you read this appendix, make sure that you're familiar with the different kinds of SAP R/3 business documents explained in Lesson 22.

QUALITY MANAGEMENT

Quality Management covers the processes of inspection and recording and analyzing inspection results. The main documents used in QM include the purchase order, production order, goods receipt, and inspection lot.

Reaching Quality Management Help For help on Quality Management, choose Help, Help Library, Materials Management, and then scroll down to Quality Management.

Inspection is closely tied in with quality management. SAP R/3 uses three basic "inspection terms" in the QM module:

- *The Inspection Catalog*—Groupsinformation about materials such as attributes, possible defects, defect causes, and so on. It's a hierarchical list, matching similar characteristics. Various combinations of characteristics may be useful at different companies.

* *The Inspection Plan*—Contains master inspection characteristics, inspection catalog data, and inspection methods.

 Master Inspection Characteristics   Can include such characteristics as weight, color, surface finish, and so on.

* *An Inspection Lot*—Can stand alone or can be created as part of an inspection plan (see Figure B.1). Inspection results are recorded only for inspections done with an inspection plan. If you want to record inspection results based on inspection characteristics, you need to assign an inspection plan.

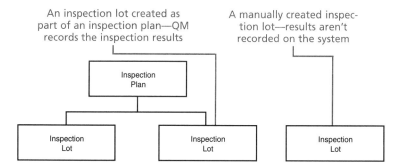

FIGURE B.1   An inspection lot can stand alone or be part of an inspection plan.

The flow chart in Figure B.2 shows a typical sequence that illustrates what QM does. It's just one way QM could work at your plant. The setup at your plant could be different from this example.

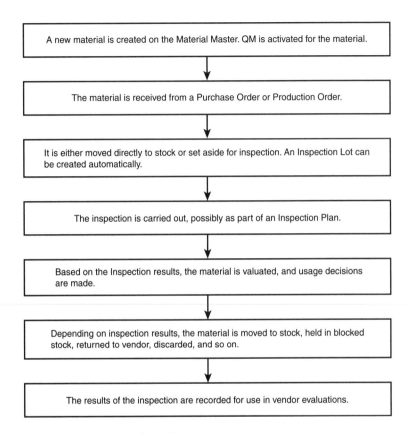

FIGURE B.2   A typical flow for Quality Management.

Quality Management can be set up (on the Material Master) in one of three ways: no quality management, quality management in procurement, or quality management with inspection processing. QM provides many features to help you manage the quality of your goods:

- QM controls movement of goods in and out of inspection stock for both procurement and inspection processing.

- With procurement, you can block activity for quality reasons at several stages. Quotation, purchase order, and goods receipt can all be blocked. You can also block purchase of one material from a vendor or all materials from a vendor.

- QM can also help you evaluate vendors, manage quality certificates, and set up quality assurance agreements and technical delivery terms.

- With inspection processing, QM controls inspection lot creation, sample drawing, recording of results, and usage decisions.

- Dynamic modification allows automatic adjustments of the sample sizes and inspection plans based on the quality level. For example, a recent lower quality performance would trigger more rigorous inspections.

- The Quality Management module is *ISO 9004*–compliant, including inspection planning, internal quality audits, quality system documentation, statistical sampling, test equipment, material traceability, and quality costs.

ISO 9004   An international quality standard defining processes a company must use to be certified. Many buyers now require their vendors and suppliers to be ISO 9000 certified.

PLANT MAINTENANCE

The Plant Maintenance (PM) module helps you plan and control both preventative maintenance and repair of your production facilities and equipment. If your requirements vary from job to job (from planned retooling to emergency repairs, for example), you can use many of the tools in some cases and fewer in others.

Help with Plant Maintenance   For help on Plant Maintenance, choose Help, Help Library, Plant Maintenance. Be advised, however, that when the Help files refer to technical objects, they mean pieces of equipment or a plant location.

You must understand two key concepts to learn how the technical information about your plant is structured:

- *Functional location*—The place in your process where equipment is installed. Two examples of functional locations in Figure B.3 are Number 2 Steam Plant Boiler Feedwater Pump and Number 2 Boiler Gas Burner. A functional location can have many pieces of equipment installed.

- *Equipment*—A physical piece of machinery purchased on a certain date with specific warranty information and a serial number. An example of this is the 500 HP GE 3 phase motor, serial #57200857, bought in September 1989. (Equipment can be moved between similar functional locations or be kept in inventory as spare.) Equipment can be made up of several other pieces of equipment.

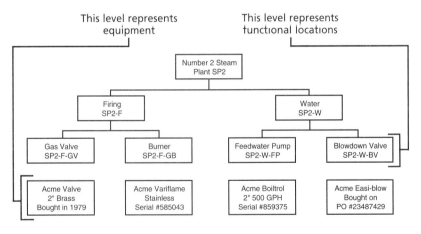

FIGURE B.3   This is one way the locations and equipment in your plant might be structured. Again, your plant may be set up differently.

Figure B.4 shows a typical workflow for one way that PM could deal with an equipment breakdown. Your workflow might vary, depending on your plant and the urgency of the repair.

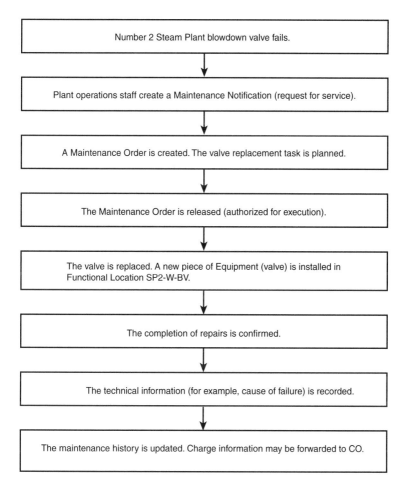

FIGURE B.4   A typical flow for Preventative Maintenance.

Some general PM information:

- The main documents necessary for PM are maintenance notification (which notes that something is broken) and maintenance order (which says "Go fix this").

- The main master files involved are Functional Location, Equipment Master, and Bill of Materials.

- PM can communicate to MM to take material from stock. It can also contact Human Resources for timekeeping and Controlling for charge information.

- Using functional location and equipment helps you find causes for problems. For example, it can highlight if a particular functional location is a problem area, or if equipment from a certain vendor is giving you trouble.

- You can assign maintenance tasks to both internal and external groups.

- To really leverage your information in PM, you need to have the people who repaired the equipment (the tradespeople) record their technical findings. These include such items as component damaged, kind of damage, cause of damage, and actions taken to correct.

HUMAN RESOURCES

Human Resources (HR) takes care of payroll, time recording, applicant administration, and organizational data. You can represent many different kinds of organizational structures in HR. Figure B.5 shows a sample company structure that you could create in HR.

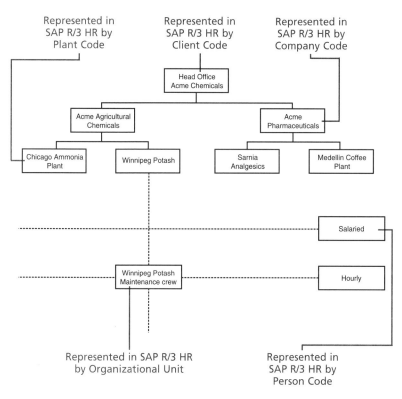

FIGURE B.5   One way of representing a company structure in SAP R/3.

 HR Help   For help with Human Resources, choose Help, Help Library, Human Resources.

Many processes are involved in HR, and many activities are related to organization and structure. Probably the most basic (and near and dear to our hearts) is payroll. The flow chart in Figure B.6 shows a typical payroll sequence.

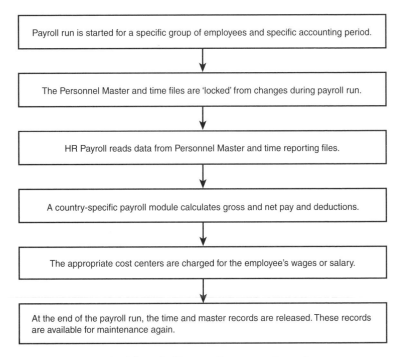

FIGURE B.6   A typical flow in Human Resources Payroll.

Some general functions of HR include the following:

- Tracking and controlling travel expenses and meeting room reservations.

- Accepting input from an external time recording system.

- Handling negative and positive time recording. In a negative time recording system, HR assumes that the employee is working her scheduled shift, and subtracts any reported exceptions to this. In a positive time recording system, HR assumes that the employee works only the hours he specifically reports.

- Taking retroactive adjustments into account.

- Referencing holiday schedules for different employee groups.

- Using the Personnel Master File.

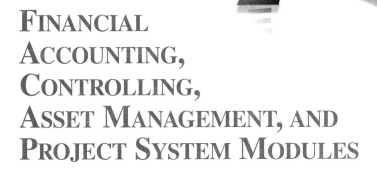

Appendix C

Financial Accounting, Controlling, Asset Management, and Project System Modules

Financial Accounting

Financial Accounting (FI) includes Accounts Payable, Accounts Receivable, Credit Management, Treasury, Financial Information System, General Ledger (G/L), and Extended G/L.

 SAP R/3 Accounting Modules FI and Controlling (CO) are set up so that just one entry is required for each business transaction. There's no need to copy records from one subledger to another.

The General Ledger provides a complete picture of all business transactions (see Figure C.1). It gets its data from automatic postings from subledgers. All G/L numbers are tied to source documents. From the G/L level, you can zoom progressively to more detail until you get to the actual source document. The G/L collects all the accounts.

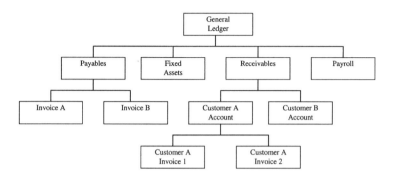

FIGURE C.1   One way a company structure can be set up in FI.

The flow chart in Figure C.2 illustrates a typical workflow for selling a product and receiving payment, which is FI's primary role in the sale of a product.

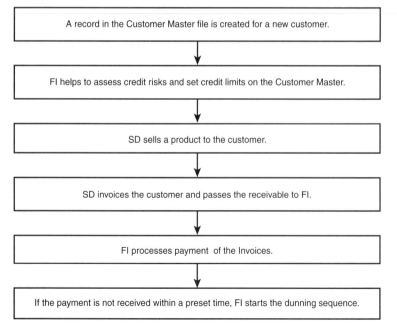

FIGURE C.2   A typical flow in Financial Accounting.

Financial Accounting Help   For help on Financial Accounting, choose Help, Help Library, Financial Accounting.

Using SAP R/3's FI module is also beneficial for these reasons:

- Flexible closing reports are available for daily, monthly, and yearly periods.

- Non–SAP R/3 sources and data destinations can be accommodated by using Automatic Procedures to batch data in or out. This allows you to interface SAP R/3 to existing systems in your organization where required.

- The Financial Information System helps you evaluate customers and vendors.

- You can use Consolidation to aggregate the results from individual companies to a group of companies.

The main documents used in FI include invoices (in and out), credit notes, payments, and G/L. The main master files used in FI are Vendor and Customer. FI interfaces to MM purchasing for Accounts Payable and to SD sales for Accounts Receivable.

CONTROLLING

In the Controlling (CO) module, the cost accounting is carried out within a *controlling area*. This isn't necessarily the same as FI, which presents accounts at a company code level. Figure C.3 shows a business setup for CO.

Controlling Area   A grouping that can be used to aggregate the control of several distinct companies.

These two levels set up by FI   This level set up by CO

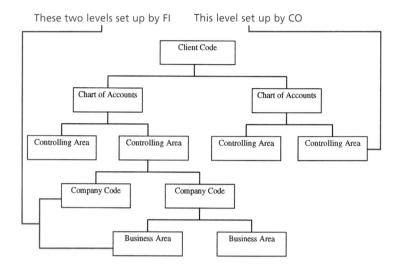

FIGURE C.3   One way a company structure could be set up in CO.

The following statements will help you better understand CO:

- A controlling area can contain one or more company codes.

- A company code represents a legal entity. A business area is a lower division and is used only for internal accounting.

- CO does Cost Center Accounting (CCA) and Profit Center Accounting (PCA). Costs are allocated to the appropriate accounts.

Controlling Help   For help on Controlling, choose Help, Help Library, Controlling.

To illustrate a typical flow in CO, Figure C.4 shows how an organization could manage its telephone cost center to allocate telephone costs across cost centers.

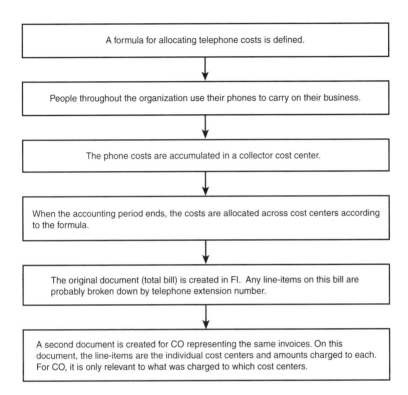

A formula for allocating telephone costs is defined.

People throughout the organization use their phones to carry on their business.

The phone costs are accumulated in a collector cost center.

When the accounting period ends, the costs are allocated across cost centers according to the formula.

The original document (total bill) is created in FI. Any line-items on this bill are probably broken down by telephone extension number.

A second document is created for CO representing the same invoices. On this document, the line-items are the individual cost centers and amounts charged to each. For CO, it is only relevant to what was charged to which cost centers.

FIGURE C.4   A typical flow in Controlling.

CO also performs the following functions in SAP R/3:

- Tracks product costing and process costing

- Provides Profitability Analysis and Executive Information System

Executive Information System   A system used to monitor key indicators that executives use to "take the pulse" of their businesses. The indicators chosen vary from business to business. Facilities in which to look at the detailed data are usually also provided.

- Makes available periodic and on-demand reports
- Offers Business Planning and Control, Internal Orders, and Open Item Management

CO creates very little original documentation—it collects, groups, and charges source documents originating in other modules. The major documentation concepts used in CO are Cost Centers, Profit Centers, and Cost Elements. CO interfaces to General Ledger and the Asset Management module. Input is also drawn from FI and MM.

ASSET MANAGEMENT

Asset Management (AM) provides tools to acquire, depreciate, evaluate, and retire assets. The kinds of assets covered are fixed, low value, leased, and real estate.

- Low value assets depreciate in the year they are bought and are often aggregated as a single asset master record.

- Depreciation often needs to be tracked (for more than one reason), so SAP R/3 enables you to depreciate the same piece of equipment in several parallel ways.

- SAP R/3 can represent company structure for AM in several ways. Charts of Depreciation can be at the same organizational level as Charts of Accounts, or depreciation can be a sublevel from Charts of Accounts (as shown in Figure C.5).

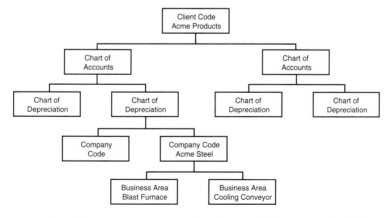

FIGURE C.5   One way a company structure could be set up in AM.

Figure C.6 shows how AM manages an asset through its useful life (the asset's life cycle).

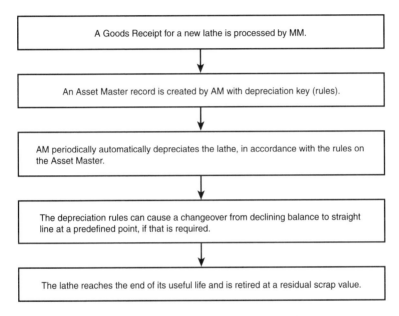

A Goods Receipt for a new lathe is processed by MM.

An Asset Master record is created by AM with depreciation key (rules).

AM periodically automatically depreciates the lathe, in accordance with the rules on the Asset Master.

The depreciation rules can cause a changeover from declining balance to straight line at a predefined point, if that is required.

The lathe reaches the end of its useful life and is retired at a residual scrap value.

FIGURE C.6   A typical flow of an Asset through its lifetime.

The main transactions used in AM are Acquisition, Capitalization, Transfer, Depreciation, and Retirement. The main master data includes Chart of Depreciation and Asset Master.

When an asset is acquired, it can be brought into SAP with Create Asset. Asset Management can also transfer cost planning information to Controlling, and Asset Management can produce lists of ordered goods by location or room number to ease taking physical inventory or assets.

PROJECT SYSTEM

Project System (PS) helps you to plan, manage, control, and track the costs of R&D projects, marketing projects, software projects, made-to-order products, and so on. The common tasks revolve around allocation of people, resources, and money within the framework of schedule and task relationships.

Accessing Project System You can access Project System from two different menu paths: Logistics, Project Management or Accounting, Project Management.

Help on Project System In the help library, PS is part of CO. For help on Project System, choose Help, Help Library, Controlling, and then scroll down to Project System.

You break your project into logical subdivisions and represent it in a *work breakdown structure* (WBS). You can then divide the WBS by phases, assemblies, subsystems, or whatever makes sense for your specific project (see Figure C.7).

Work Breakdown Structure A development step designed to assist you in working out task lists, relationships, costs, and so on. The WBS will evolve and become more detailed as your project progresses.

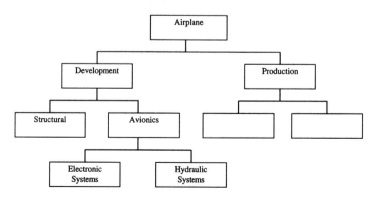

FIGURE C.7   A sample WBS for a new aircraft.

The flow chart in Figure C.8 illustrates one way you could use PS to plan, execute, and control a project.

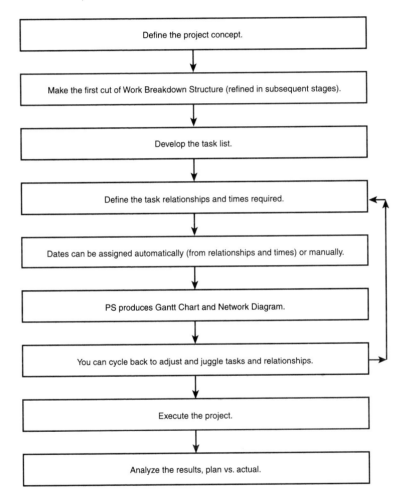

FIGURE C.8   A typical sequence for executing a project.

This list summarizes some advantages of using PS:

- Throughout the project phases, actual (as opposed to planned) costs and dates are fed back into the model. A Project Information System is available for tracking results to date. (You can also track project costing in various ways.)

- You can use the SAP R/3 Documentation Management System to track project documentation (document owner, location, and so on).

- Both capacity planning and cost planning are available in PS.

- Availability can be confirmed on Materials and on Production Resources and Tools.

- PS can control and track work assigned to outside resources.

- You can do *loop* analysis on your task networks with PS.

 Loop   A sequence of tasks in which you can follow the prerequisites back and end up having a future task as a prerequisite for a past one. PS will help you exorcise these demons if they sneak into your project plan.

The main document elements involved in PS are the Work Breakdown Structure, *Gantt Chart*, Network Diagram, Activities (tasks), and Bill of Materials. When you use PS, you can make postings to CO, confirm materials through MM, and verify production resources and tools with PP.

 Gantt Chart   Lists tasks down the left side, ordered by start date. The bottom of the chart lists the weeks or months. Horizontal bars represent the length of each task.

Exchanging Project Data You can exchange SAP R/3 project data with Microsoft Project by using the .mpx format. If you are in the middle of a project and decide to change project management tools, you can move your data into the new environment.

INDEX

J-K-L

Q-R

S